The Classic Collection

JIFFY NEEDLE TATTING
•HOLIDAY COLLECTION•

By Selma and Ed Morin

KC Publishing, Inc.

700 W. 47th Street, Suite 310 • Kansas City, Missouri 64112

JIFFY NEEDLE TATTING

ATTENTION: SCHOOLS AND BUSINESS FIRMS
KC Publishing, Inc. books are available at quantity discounts for bulk purchases for educational, business or sales promotional use. Inquiries should be directed to our Book Sales Department at (816) 531-5730.

Printed in the United States of America

LIBRARY OF CONGRESS CATALOGING-IN-PUBLICATION DATA

Morin, Selma.
    Jiffy Needle Tatting: Holiday Collection/by Selma and Ed Morin.
       p. cm. − (The Classic Collection)
    Includes index.
    ISBN: 0-86675-342-7
    1. Tatting I. Morin, Ed. II. Title. III. Series: Classic Collection (Kansas City, Mo.)
  TT840.T38M67 1992   92-30113
  746.43'6 − dc20   CIP

TABLE OF CONTENTS

HOLIDAY PATTERNS

ABOUT THE AUTHORS

Edward A. Morin holds three master's degrees in the field of educational administration and counseling and has worked at the elementary, secondary and college levels. His wife, Selma L. Morin, has a master's degree in social work and has worked in administration on the university level as well as at both state and county levels of social services. She is a subject of biographical record in *Who's Who of American Women.* The Morin's are now retired and living in Portland, Oregon.

INTRODUCTION

Tatting is an ancient needlecraft that was practiced in Europe and the Far East for centuries. By the 1700s European nobility had taken up the art because they wanted ornate laces for garments and edgings. The Pilgrims brought this graceful form of needlework to America and it remained popular until World War I. In recent years, there has been a renewed interest in learning this ancient art.

Reduced to its simplest form, tatting is nothing more than tying knots (double stitches) over a thread or carrying cord. The result is a delicate lace with numerous uses, ranging from beautiful edgings for handkerchiefs to decorative insertions for afghans.

Traditional tatting uses a shuttle and/or ball. Because learning to shuttle tat requires a unique finger and hand dexterity, shuttle tatting has always had a small following with needlecrafters. Now there is a new way, a quicker and easier way, with the same beautiful results — Jiffy Needle Tatting!

Selma Morin wanted very much to learn to shuttle tat as a child, but because Selma was blind, her mother, an accomplished tatter, was unable to teach her. When Selma went away to Perkins Institute for the Blind in Watertown, Massachusetts, she successfully learned to crochet, knit, sew and weave. However, shuttle tatting was not offered at the Institute. Before graduating Selma recovered some of her vision through surgery, but by then her mother had died and she felt that she might never learn to tat.

The opportunity to learn to shuttle tat didn't present itself until Selma went to Regis College in Weston, Massachusetts. There she met a nun, who lacked the finger dexterity to shuttle tat, but understood its principals and basic concepts and was able to teach Selma. Selma believed that anyone could learn to tat, but not neccesarily using the same technique. To prove her point, she began searching for a new way to tat.

After Selma was married in 1961, her husband Edward joined the search. Together they developed a new method of tatting, using the Jiffy Tatting Needle. This new method is versatile and allows tatters to combine tatting with other needle arts...and yes, anyone can learn to tat with the Jiffy Needle!!

Here are some comments from needlecrafters about Jiffy Needle Tatting:

"I learned Jiffy Needle Tatting in only two hours after trying for months to learn shuttle tatting."

"Jiffy Needle Tatting hooked me! Anyone can learn this method — the young, senior citizens, even the handicapped."

"I am left-handed and Jiffy Needle Tatting finally allowed me to tat after many unsuccessful attempts at traditional tatting."

"Jiffy Needle Tatting is fun and easy! I only wish it had been developed many years ago!"

Jiffy Needle Tatting is not intended to replace shuttle tatting, but to expand this beautiful needle art. The needles come in nine different sizes for use with everything from delicate threads to heavy yarns. With complete how-to instructions and a delightful collection of projects, this book brings the joy of tatting to everyone — even those who have been unable to learn traditional shuttle tatting!

BASIC INSTRUCTIONS

PREPARATION

MATERIALS NEEDED

A knitting gauge is helpful to check the size of medium and large tatting needles. You will also need scissors and an embroidery needle to work in ends of the threads and fine yarns and a yarn needle to work in yarns used with the larger tatting needles.

Use a fine thread of the same color for a carrying cord if tatted double stitches on the small steel tatting needles are too difficult to slide off onto the carrying cord.

To learn the initial techniques of needle tatting, a Jiffy Tatting Needle #2 is most versatile. However, you will want all sizes to complete all of the patterns in this book.

TATTING TIPS

Follow the instructions given on label of thread or yarn for laundering. Hand launder, or if machine washable, place item in a mesh bag. Spin dry and lay flat to complete drying.

To ensure understanding and remembering the instructions, examine each illustration carefully and read each step aloud or have someone read them to you as you learn to needle tat.

INSTRUCTIONS ON INITIAL TECHNIQUES

TATTING A RING

You will need a Size 2 Jiffy Tatting Needle (JTN) and appropriate yarn, scissors and a yarn needle. Cut a strand of yarn 1-1/2 yards long, fold it in half to make a double strand carrying cord (cc). **Always fold the yarn in half to make the carrying cord unless otherwise instructed.**

The carrying cord holds all the knots first made on the Jiffy Tatting Needle (JTN). It is doubled to facilitate the closing and locking of tatted rings (r) in

---

SUGGESTED THREADS AND YARNS

SMALL

0000 DMC Size 12 Pearl Cotton for ball strand and No. 70 Tatting Thread for the carrying cord

000 DMC Size 8 Pearl Cotton for ball strand and Size 12 for the carrying cord

00 DMC Size 5 Pearl Cotton for ball strand and Size 8 for the carrying cord

MEDIUM

0 DMC Size 3 Pearl Cotton

1 Fingering and Fine Knitting Machine Yarns

2 Baby Yarn and Fine Sports Weight Yarns

LARGE

3 Heavy Sports Weight Fine 4-Ply Worsted Yarns

4 Heavier 4-Ply Weight Yarns

5 Rug Yarns (nubby, fringed or looped yarns are not recommended nor any yarn which has a great amount of stretch)

Note: Jiffy Tatting Needles sizes 0 to 5 all use the same size thread or yarn as the ball strand for the carrying cord.

place, as well as making the work more supple. Also, any twist is easily seen in a double carrying cord (cc) and can be easily corrected by giving the Jiffy Tatting Needle (JTN) a twist in the opposite direction to straighten the carrying cord (cc) and continue tatting.

A single carrying cord (cc) is not recommended because it is more difficult to close the first ring (r) or to stabilize the double stitches (ds) while tatting. It also fails to give the correct "cushy" feel to the work, particularly when tatting with yarn. A twist in a single carry-

ABBREVIATIONS

Because it is important to become familiar with the abbreviations used in tatting, in the beginning of this book abbreviations will be added after the written-out wording. Later, written-out words and phrases will be reduced to the abbreviations so you can become familiar with reading pattern instructions as they appear in the projects that follow and in all tatting books. The terms are listed alphabetically for easy reference.

bp	Beaded picot
cc	Carrying cord
ch	Chain(s)
clr	Close ring
ds	Double stitch(s)
dsb	Double stitch backwards
fhh	First half hitch
j	Join
jk	Josephine Knot
JTN	Jiffy Tatting Needle
lp	Long picot
mp	Measured picot
p	Picot(s)
r	Ring(s)
rnd	Round
rnp	Run Jiffy Tatting Needle through picot and back through carrying cord
rnr	Run Jiffy Tatting Needle through base of ring and back through carrying cord
sep	Separated
shh	Second half hitch

sk	Skip
sson	Slide stitches off needle
st	Stitch(s)
s-1b	Slip one bead
tog	Together
tp	Tiny picot(s)
*	Repeat from asterisk

Since some patterns in this book combine Jiffy Needle Tatting with other needle arts, the following knit and crochet abbreviations are used:

Knit

dec	Decrease
inc	Increase
k	Knit
p	Purl
sl st	Slip stitch
sk	Skip
st	Stitch
tog	Together
yo	Yarn Over

Crochet

ch	Chain
dc	Double crochet
dec	Decrease
hdc	Half double crochet
inc	Increase
sc	Single crochet
sk	Skip
sl st	Slip stitch
st	Stitch
yo	Yarn over

ing cord (cc) is not easily seen and can cause tatting problems. For finer Jiffy Tatting Needles (JTN) you will find a needle threader helpful. When using a needle threader, insert end of threader through eye of the Jiffy Tatting Needle (JTN) and catch the two ends of the double strand of carrying cord (cc) (see Figure 1). Pull threader back out of Jiffy Tatting Needle (JTN) eye, bringing through both ends of the carrying cord (cc). Remove threader.

Threaded tatting needle is held in the right hand with the loop hanging down at the other end of the carrying cord (cc). Tatted knots are formed on the left thumb with the yarn from the ball or skein before they are worked onto the Jiffy Tatting Needle (JTN). The tatted knot is a double stitch (ds) composed of two half hitches and made as follows: Pick up an end of yarn from the ball or skein with the left hand and place it under the right thumb, holding it against the tatting needle in the right hand; leave a 3-inch length (or tail). Slide the left hand down about eight inches on

ball strand and hold yarn with the fingers leaving thumb free (see Figures 2, 3 and 4).

While holding threaded tatting needle with right hand, wrap ball strand around left thumb in a clockwise direction (see Figure 3). Insert tip of needle under the loop on outside of thumb. Slide tip up along outside edge of thumb and lift off first half hitch (fhh), sliding it onto the needle (see Figure 4). Remove left thumb and pull ball strand with left hand to slide first half hitch (fhh) next to right thumb and to tighten it on needle. Do not move right thumb or index finger (see Figure 5).

While still holding ball strand with fingers of left hand and the Jiffy Tatting Needle (JTN) in the right hand, wrap ball strand with right hand around left thumb in counterclockwise direction to form second half hitch (shh) of the double stitch (ds) (see Figure 6). Insert tip of needle inside the thumb, behind and under the back of the loop on thumb. Tip should be pointing toward the left thumb. Slide tip up along inside edge of

Fig. 1   Fig. 3   Fig. 5

Fig. 2   Fig. 4   Fig. 6

thumb and lift off second half hitch (shh) of double stitch (ds) onto needle (see Figure 7).

Remove left thumb and pull ball strand with left hand to slide this second half hitch (shh) next to first half hitch (fhh) on needle and pull taut. This locks knot in place and completes the basic tatting knot called a double stitch (ds). Now relax the right thumb and index finger (see Figure 8). Make three more double stitches (ds) on the needle.

PICOT

Picots are small loops that stand out from the edges of the rings (r) and chains (ch). They are decorative and make the tatting look lacy. They are also used to join (j) rings (r) and chains (ch) to form designs and motifs. A picot (p) is easy to make on the Jiffy Tatting Needle (JTN).

A fingertip picot (p), referred to as a tiny picot (tp), is made by spacing the knots 1/4 inch on the needle. For a picot (p), place the tip of right index finger on the needle in front of last double stitch (ds) made. Holding the finger in place, tat the first half of the double stitch (ds) (see Figure 9). Complete second half of double stitch (ds) and remove finger. The space is about 1/4 inch wide. Slide double stitch (ds) next to previous double stitch (ds) on needle; hanging yarn forms a loop.

A picot (p) refers only to this loop and does not count as a double stitch (ds). This picot (p) is counted with the double stitch (ds) which follows the picot (p) (see Figure 10.) Refer to special techniques in Chapter III for making twin picots (p).

Continue to complete the ring (r) by tatting three double stitches (ds). Place fingertip on needle for a second picot (p) and tat four more double stitches (ds). Place fingertip on needle for a third picot (p) and end with tatting four double stitches (ds). The tatting on your needle should look like Figure 11.

Cradle work in the **left** hand between thumb and first two fingers and grasp the tip of Jiffy Tatting Needle (JTN)

Fig. 7   Fig. 9   Fig. 11

Fig. 8   Fig. 10   Fig. 12

with the right hand (see Figure 12). Pull the needle up with the **right** hand, drawing the carrying cord (cc) through the double stitch (ds), and then slide off needle onto carrying cord (cc). Continue sliding double stitch (ds) to within two inches from looped end of carrying cord (cc). While still holding double stitch (ds) with left hand, insert tip of Jiffy Tatting Needle (JTN) through looped end of carrying cord (cc) (see Figure 13).

Pull needle and front end of carrying cord (cc) through loop and exert a little pressure with fingers and thumb of left hand on last few double stitches (ds) to guide the stitches. Continue pulling carrying cord (cc) with fingers of right hand through the double stitches (ds) to secure them together (tog) to form and close ring (clr) (see Figure 14). This completes the first ring (r) (see Figure 15). **Note:** The base of the ring (r) is the point where the two ends of the row of double stitches (ds) come together to form the ring (r).

TATTING A CHAIN

Pick up ring (r) so that carrying cord (cc) is on the right and the ball strand on the left (see Figure 16). This places the ring (r) with right side facing you. This side shows all the ridges (or double stitches) around the edge of the ring in front. If you look at the back side of the ring (r), they are missing at the base of the picot (p).

*To tat a chain (ch), fold carrying cord (cc) down and across back of ring (r) with right hand. Hold Jiffy Tatting Needle (JTN) with right hand and with left hand place ring (r), right side up, under right thumb up against needle (see Figure 17). When tatting a chain (ch), the half hitches of the double stitches (ds) are **reversed**, by tatting the second half of the double stitches (ds) first (see Figure 18) and the first half last (see Figure 19). This is called a double stitch backwards (dsb). This procedure will place all ridges of the chain (ch) on the right side when the chain (ch) is completed.

To tat a chain (ch), work 6 double stitches (ds) on Jiffy Tatting Needle

Fig. 13   Fig. 15   Fig. 17

Fig. 14   Fig. 16   Fig. 18

(JTN) next to the base of previous ring (r), make a picot (p) and six more double stitches backwards (dsb) (see Figure 20). Place work in a cradled position of left hand, between thumb and first two fingers (see Figure 12).

Straighten out carrying cord (cc) falling through left hand. Pull needle up with right hand. This draws carrying cord (cc) through double stitches backwards (dsb) as they slide off needle onto carrying cord (cc) until they are in position next to the tatted ring (r). The double stitches backwards (dsb) have formed a semi-circle shaped chain (ch) with the picot (p) facing up (see Figure 21).

There is no visible ridge at the base of the picot (p) on this side of the chain (ch). With the fingers of right hand, turn chain (ch) toward you and down. This is called reversing the chain. It brings all of the ridges on the chain (ch) to the right side to match the ring (r) and places the chain (ch) in the correct position to tat the next ring (r) (see Figure 22).

TATTING A SECOND RING

Place the Jiffy Tatting Needle (JTN) on top of last double stitch (ds) of chain (ch) just made and hold both chain (ch) and needle firmly in place between thumb and fingers of right hand (see Figure 23). Tat a ring (r) of four double stitches (ds) on Jiffy Tatting Needle (JTN) next to the chain (ch). Instead of making a picot (p), join (j) to last picot (p) in previous ring (r) (this is a shared picot) as follows: To join (j) to picot (p), hold previous ring (r) in left hand below tip of needle. Insert tip of needle down into third or last picot (p) of ring (r) referred to as previous ring (r). The thread length in the ring (r) is at lower left. Place ball strand over tip of needle to catch and draw it back through picot (p) as a loop, a slip or a knit stitch and leave it on needle — it does not count as a stitch (st). Lightly pull ball strand to tighten and place it next to last double stitch (ds) on needle (see Figure 24).

Continue to complete ring (r) by tatting four double stitches (ds), picot (p),

Fig. 19   Fig. 21   Fig. 23

Fig. 20   Fig. 22   Fig. 24

four double stitches (ds), picot (p), four double stitches (ds) (see Figure 25). Cradle work in left hand between thumb and fingers (see Figure 12). Straighten and separate (sep) carrying cord (cc) in left hand. Pull needle up with right hand, drawing the carrying cord (cc) through double stitches (ds) and sliding stitches off needle (sson), onto carrying cord (cc). Continue pulling carrying cord (cc) to slide stitches (st) within two inches of end of previous chain (ch).

Notice the two loops made by the carrying cord (cc). Insert the tip of needle through **only one loop of carrying cord** (cc) (see Figure 26). Pull needle with carrying cord (cc) through the loop and continue pulling carrying cord (cc) with fingers of right hand to gather and lock the double stitches (ds) in place and to close (see Figure 27).

Repeat from asterisk (*) at the Chain Section to continue tatting a row of chains (ch) and rings (r). This simple edging can be made with all of the tatting needles and appropriate thread or yarn to trim a variety of articles.

INSTRUCTIONS ON ADDITIONAL TECHNIQUES

JOINING A NEW CARRYING CORD

It is easier to add or piece a new cc after a r has been completed. Unthread tatting needle and thread with a **new** cc. Set aside. Thread a yarn needle with both ends of the **old** cc. Insert threaded yarn needle through looped end of **new** cc. Work in ends of the **old** cc back through and around about 3/4 of the "tubing" of the ds on back side of previous r to secure new cc in place and trim ends (see Figure 28).

ADDING A NEW BALL OR SKEIN

It is easier to add a new ball or skein after a r has been completed. Hold threaded JTN with right hand. Let tatted work rest on your lap or a table (see Figure 29). Place end of new ball or skein against needle under the thumb, leaving a 3-inch length. Follow instructions for tatting the ch beginning at * in the

Fig. 25   Fig. 27   Fig. 29

Fig. 26   Fig. 28   Fig. 30

Chain Section (see Figures 18, 19, 20, 21 and 22).

Place strip on table right side down so ch are on left with last ch away from you. Use a needle to work in ends, one at a time, into back side of work. The old end from r is worked into knots of new ch and the new end from the ch is worked into the knots of old r; trim ends. To resume tatting, turn work over to the right so last ch will be on the right and last r on left (Figure 23 shows correct position).

CORRECTING MISTAKES

If the mistake is on the needle, slide the ds off front end of needle to where the mistake occurred and resume tatting. If mistake is in the work, unthread the JTN and insert tip of needle between the knots to catch and pull out cc between each r and ch until mistake is removed. Rethread the JTN and resume tatting.

TATTING A SECOND ROW AND JOINING TECHNIQUES

After tatting a straight row of r and ch, next learn how to build on an existing row. It is important to remember that the row will be straight and the ds in the ch are usually about 3/4 the ds in a r. For example, if the r has 16 ds, the ch will have 12 dsb. However, when the pattern calls for a p in the center of the ch, the dsb stitches will be ch 6 dsb, p, 6 dsb, sson. There are three ways to tat rows together: (1) The rings of the second row are joined to the chains of the first row. (2) The rings of the second row are joined to the rings of the first row. (3) The chains of the second row are joined to the chains of the first row.

JOINING RINGS OF SECOND ROW TO CHAINS OF FIRST ROW

Row 1: Tat a row of 4 r and 3 ch as fol-
lows: Thread JTN with 1-1/2 yards of yarn for cc. R of 4 ds, 3 p sep by 4 ds, 4 ds, sson, clr. *Ch 6 dsb, p, 6 dsb, sson. R of 4 ds, j to last p of previous r, 4 ds, p, 4 ds, p, 4 ds, sson, clr. Repeat from * twice. Remove JTN and work in ends. Place first row down on table with r pointing toward you right side up — right side shows knot ridges at base of p (see Figure 30).

Row 2: Thread JTN with 1-1/2 yards of yarn for cc. R of 4 ds, p, 4 ds, pick up ch at the right end of first row and j to p, 4 ds, p, 4 ds, sson, clr. *Ch 6 dsb, p, 6 dsb, sson. R of 4 ds, j to last p of previous r, 4 ds, j to p in next ch in previous row, 4 ds, p, 4 ds, sson, clr. Repeat from * once. Note: This row is shorter than previous row because in a row of r and ch of this type there is always one r more than ch in the row (see Figure 30). This method is used for simple tatted triangles.

JOINING RINGS TO CHAINS RESULTING IN EVEN ROW LENGTHS

Row 1: Thread JTN with 1-1/2 yards of yarn for cc. R of 3 ds, 4 p sep by 2 ds, 3 ds, sson, clr. *Ch 3 dsb, p, 3 dsb, p, 3 dsb, sson. R of 3 ds, j to last p of previous r, 2 ds, 3 p sep by 2 ds, 3 ds, sson, clr. Repeat from * twice. Remove JTN, work in ends and trim. Place piece on table right side up with r pointing toward you.

Row 2: Thread JTN with 1-1/2 yards of yarn for cc. R of 3 ds, p, 2 ds, p, 2 ds. Pick up first ch on right and j to first p, 2 ds, p, 3 ds, sson, clr. *Ch 3 dsb, p, 3 dsb, p, 3 dsb, sson. R of 3 ds, j to last p of previous r, 2 ds, j to last p in same ch of previous row, 2 ds, j to first p in next ch of previous row, 2 ds, p, 3 ds, sson, clr. Repeat from * once. Ch 3 dsb, p, 3 dsb, p, 3 dsb, sson, ending r of 3 ds, j to last p of previous r, 2 ds, j to last p in same ch of previous row, 2 ds, p, 2 ds, p, 3 ds, sson, clr. In this method of joining rings to chains, the rings bridge the chains. The rings of the second row are also in line with the rings of the previous row (see Figure 31). This method is used for covering large areas.

JOINING RINGS OF SECOND ROW TO RINGS OF FIRST ROW

Row 1: Thread JTN with 1-1/2 yards yarn for cc. R of 4 ds, 3 p sep by 4 ds, 4 ds, sson, clr. *Ch 6 dsb, p, 6 dsb, sson. R of 4 ds, j to last p of previous r, 4 ds, p, 4 ds, p, 4 ds, sson, clr. Repeat from * twice. Remove JTN, work in ends and trim. Place piece on table so ch are right side up. Rethread JTN.

Row 2: R of 4 ds, p, 4 ds, j to middle p of r at right end of first row, 4 ds, p, 4 ds, sson, clr. *Ch 6 dsb, p, 6 dsb, sson. R of 4 ds, j to last p of previous r, 4 ds, j to middle p of next r of previous row, 4 ds, p, 4 ds, sson, clr. Repeat from * twice. Remove JTN, work in ends and trim (see Figure 32). Omitting picots from chains in tatting straight rows results in a nice motif for belts and sashes. The Victoria's Belt pattern (end of this section) is an example of this motif.

JOINING CHAINS TO CHAINS

Row 1: Thread JTN with 1-1/2 yards yarn for cc. R of 4 ds, 3 p sep by 4 ds, 4 ds, sson, clr. *Ch 6 dsb, p, 6 dsb, sson. R of 4 ds, j to last p of previous r, 4 ds, p, 4 ds, p, 4 ds, sson, clr. Repeat from * twice. Remove JTN, work in ends and trim. Place piece on table right side down – wrong side shows no ridges at base of picots.

Row 2: Thread JTN with 1-1/2 yards yarn for cc. R of 4 ds, 3 p sep by 3 ds, 4 ds, sson, clr. Turn r so back faces you and middle p is pointing right. Bring cc toward you, under ball strand and across top of r toward middle p. Ch 6 dsb, j to p in first ch at right end of first row, 6 dsb, sson. Turn work counterclockwise so first row is across front of table extending right. R of second row is to the left end of previous row with the length of yarn from that r to left of r; cc is at back of work. R of 4 ds, j to last p of previous r, 4 ds, p, 4 ds, p, 4 ds, sson, clr. *Turn work clockwise, bringing cc toward you, under ball strand and across previous r. Ch 6 dsb, j to p in next ch of previous row, 6 dsb, sson, clr. Turn work counterclockwise, pulling cc to back of work; r is on left (right side facing). R of 4 ds, j to last p of previous r, 4 ds, p, 4 ds, p, 4 ds, sson, clr. Repeat from * once (see Figure 33) right side facing. Remember: When using this method of joining chains and rings to previous row that the work must be turned. This direction will be given in the pattern (see Figure 33).

Fig. 31   Fig. 32   Fig. 33

PROJECTS

Dottie's Fancy Hair Clip

A simple all-occasion hair clip that matches any outfit by changing the color of ribbon.

Materials: JTN #000 and threader, embroidery needle and scissors, piece of netting 12 x 2-1/2 inches folded as bias tape, 20 inches 3/8-inch red satin ribbon, 1/2 ball of DMC #8 white pearl cotton thread, 10 yards DMC #12 white pearl cotton thread, a safety pin and a gold colored hair clip.

Step 1: Fold netting as bias tape with raw edges on inside, pin and baste to hold in place.

Row 1: Thread JTN with 2 yards of DMC #12 for cc. Join cc to netting by running JTN through the two edges at right end of netting tape and back through loop of cc, securing cc to net-ting. *Ch 6 dsb, p, 6 dsb, sson. Overcast stitch on edge of netting 3/8 inch to the left to j ch, then run JTN between strands of cc and secure to edge. Repeat from * across netting. Remove JTN, work in ends and trim.

Row 2: Thread JTN with 2 yards of thread for cc. Beginning in same stitch at right end of netting, ch edge up and right side facing, run JTN through same first st of previous row and through loop of cc, secure to edge of netting. Ch 18 dsb, sson. R of 8 ds, j to p of first ch in previous row, 4 ds, p, 4 ds, sson, clr. *3 Dsb, 5 p sep by 2 dsb, 3 dsb, sson. R of 4 ds, j to last p of previous r, 4 ds, j to p of next ch of previous row, 4 ds, p, 4 ds, sson, clr. Repeat from * across all ch except last ch of previous row; ch 3 dsb, 5 p sep by 2 dsb, 3 dsb, sson. R of 4 ds, j to last p of previous r, 4 ds, j to p in last ch of previous row, 8 ds, sson, clr. Ch 18 dsb, sson. J ch to same st in net-ting where first ch of first row is con-nected. Run JTN through that st, between strands of cc, and secure to net-ting. Remove JTN, work in ends and trim.

Step 2: Attach pin to end of ribbon and lace through netting tape. Match ribbon ends together. Tie half-knot with ribbon, gathering netting tape, tie a bow. Attach to hair clip with needle and DMC #12 thread. Steam lightly to block.

First Lullaby

This quick-to-make little stork ornament can decorate a baby gift or be used as a tree ornament. Purchase the 1-1/2-inch doll at a miniature dollhouse store.

Materials: JTN #00 and needle threader, an embroidery needle and scis-sors, two 4-inch pieces of #22 gauge cloth covered wire, two tiny, pink satin roses from fabric store, blue thread, sewing needle, 10 inches of 5/8-inch blue ribbon, 12 yards white DMC #8 for cc, 1/4 ball white DMC #5 for tatting.

Body of Bag: The rings in the two center rows are joined together to form center strip.

Row 1: Thread JTN with 1-1/2 yards DMC #8 thread for cc. R of 3 ds, 3 p sep by 3 ds, 3 ds, sson, clr. *Ch 3 dsb, p, 3 dsb, p, 3 dsb, sson. R of 3 ds, j to last p of previous r, 3 ds, p, 3 ds, p, 3 ds, sson, clr. Repeat from * 10 times. Remove JTN, sew in ends with embroidery needle, trim. Place on table right side up.

Row 2: Thread JTN with 1-1/2 yards DMC #8 for cc. R of 3 ds, p, 3 ds, j to middle p of r at right end of previous row, 3 ds, p, 3 ds, sson, clr. *Ch 3 dsb, p, 3 dsb, p, 3 dsb, sson. R of 3 ds, j to last p of previous r, 3 ds, j to middle p of next r in previous row, 3 ds, p, 3 ds, sson, clr. Repeat from * 10 times. Remove JTN, sew in ends, trim. Place center strip on table or lap, right side up. Rows 3 and 4 are side rows where rings bridge the chains of middle strip.

Row 3: Thread JTN with 1-1/2 yards DMC #8 for cc. R of 3 ds, p, 2 ds, p, 2 ds, pick up ch (pointing away from you) at right end of center strip, j to first p of ch, 2 ds, p, 3 ds, sson, clr. *Ch 9 dsb, sson – (no picots). R of 3 ds, j to last p of previous r, 2 ds, j to p in same ch of center strip, 2 ds, j to p in next ch of center strip, 2 ds, p, 3 ds, sson, clr. Repeat from * 10 times. Remove JTN, sew in ends and trim.

Row 4: Repeat Row 3, but j to ch on opposite side of center strip. Set aside.

Satin Frame for Bag: Measure one of the cloth-covered wires and mark the midpoint. Bend both ends to that midpoint for rounded ends of frame; repeat with other piece of wire. Set aside. Cut 2-1/2 inches of ribbon. Fold ends in and tack with needle and thread. Place a wire frame in ribbon and overcast edges together to encase wire; repeat for other wire. Attach frames to ends of bag by catching the p at ends with needle and thread. Set aside.

Handles for Bag: Thread JTN with DMC #8 thread 4 times needle length for cc. Pick up bag by frame, right side facing; other frame is hanging down. Run JTN through upper right corner ring of bag, back through loop of cc and secure cc over frame on bag. With DMC #5 tat 75 dsb. As JTN fills, ease dsb off needle, sson on cc. Run JTN through r at upper left corner on same side of bag and back between strands of cc; secure handle to frame. Remove JTN and sew ends into frame. Repeat for other handle.

Attaching Miniature Roses: With needle and thread, attach a rose to each end of frame for front of bag.

Sewing Sides of Bag: Thread embroidery needle with 6 inches DMC #8, doubled, fold bag and count 5 rings down on each side of bag. Run embroidery needle through the 5th ring of front and back panels through loop of the thread to join the panels. Sew ends into rings and trim; repeat for other side. Place doll in bag.

14

Victoria's Tie Belt

This belt can be made for any size. It is composed simply of rings of one row joined to rings of another row. The instructions given are for a 28-inch waist.

Materials: JTN #0 and threader, tapestry needle and scissors, size J crochet hook, 8 skeins DMC #3 pearl cotton.

Row 1: Thread JTN with 4 yards thread for cc. R of 3 ds, 3 p sep by 3 ds, 3 ds, sson, clr. *Ch 9 dsb, sson. R of 3 ds, j to last p in previous r, 3 ds, p, 3 ds, p, 3 ds, sson, clr. Repeat from * 70 times for size 28-inch waist or repeat for length desired. Piece cc as needed. When 72 rings are completed, do not cut cc.

End of belt: **Ch 16 dsb, sson. R of 7 ds, j to last p in previous r, 2 ds, p, 7 ds, sson, clr. Ch 16 dsb, sson. Do not cut cc.

Row 2: R of 3 ds, j to last p of previous r of 3 ds, j to middle p opposite r of first row, 3 ds, p, 3 ds, sson, clr. *Ch 9 dsb, sson. R of 3 ds, j to last p in previous r, 3 ds, j to middle p in next opposite r of first row, 3 ds, p, 3 ds, sson, clr. Repeat from * 70 times. Repeat from ** to complete other end of belt.

Tassel: Cut last skein in half. From remaining thread, cut two 18-inch strands, set aside. Cut excess thread same length as half skeins and add to cut halves. *Insert crochet hook in ring at one end of belt and draw through one end of a half skein. Fold ends together. Double an 18-inch strand thread through needle so ends are up at eye of the needle. Wrap loop end around skein ends to form tassel. Run needle through loop to secure. Wind doubled strand around tassel and stitch into wrapped thread to secure tassel. Repeat from * for tassel at other end of belt.

MAKING MEDALLIONS AND SQUARE MOTIFS

A major part of tatting is the construction of medallions and motifs. Often they are joined to form place mats, dresser scarves or tablecloths. A square motif is actually round with four corners squared off. Medallions consist of three main types. (1) A medallion that is actually a circle with a space in the center. (2) A medallion worked around a pivotal picot. (3) A medallion worked around a center ring.

A MEDALLION WITH A SPACE IN THE CENTER

This medallion is actually a circle of tatted rings and chains. The rings can be on the inside or on the outside of the circle.

Medallion with Rings on Inside of Circle: Thread JTN #4 with 2 yards of 4-ply yarn for cc. R of 5 ds, p, 2 ds, p, 5 ds, sson, clr. *Ch 3 dsb, 5 p sep by 2 dsb, 3 dsb, sson. R of 5 ds, j to last p of previous r, 2 ds, p, 5 ds, sson, clr. Repeat from * 3 times. Ch 3 dsb, 5 p sep by 2 dsb, 3 dsb, sson. R of 5 ds, j to last p of previous r, 2 ds, j to first p of first r, 5 ds, sson, clr. Ch 3 dsb, 5 p sep by 2 dsb, 3 dsb, sson. Run JTN up center of first r, between strands of cc, and secure cc to base of r. Remove JTN, sew in ends and trim.

In this type of medallion (see Figure 34) chains are made longer and have more double stitches than the usual 3/4 number of knots in a ring. This is because the chains curve around a wider circle than the rings. This medallion can be used as a little wreath when made of green, white or red yarn with a bow attached. It can be joined to more medallions to form a rectangle or straight line because it has an even number of chains, two on two sides and one on each of the other sides — (see end of this section for combining these medallions).

Medallion with Chains on Inside of Circle: Thread JTN with 2 yards yarn for cc. R of 2 ds, 7 p sep by 2 ds, 2 ds, sson, clr. Ch 5 dsb, sson. **R of 2 ds, j to last p of previous r. *2 Ds, p, repeat from * 5 times, 2 ds, sson, clr. Ch 5 dsb, sson.

Repeat from ** 4 times. R of 2 ds, j to last p of previous r. *2 Ds, p, repeat from * 4 times. Bring first r around to JTN counterclockwise so right side of r faces you and length of r is at top left. Join as if to clasp a necklace to the first p nearest the length of that r, 2 ds, sson, clr. Ch 5 dsb, sson. Run JTN up center of first r, back between strands of cc, and secure to base of first r. Remove JTN, sew in ends and trim (see Figure 35).

This medallion has 7 rings on the outside of the circle and can be used as a snowflake when made with JTN #0 and DMC #3 or as a Christmas wreath when made with green, white or red 4-ply yarn and attaching a bow. Several of these medallions can be worked into a round doily; to work medallions into a rectangle, make 8 rings.

MEDALLION AROUND A PIVOTAL PICOT

The pivotal picot can be either in a ring or a chain. The two following examples will illustrate one of each type.

A Pivotal Picot for a Center of Rings is a Longer Picot in First Ring of Medallion: Thread JTN with 1-1/2 yards yarn for cc. R of 3 ds, p, 5 ds, make 3/4-inch-long pivotal picot when open on the JTN, 5 ds, p, 3 ds, sson, clr. Ch 6 dsb, p, 6 dsb, sson.

*R of 3 ds, j to p of previous large r, ds, p, 3 ds, sson, clr. Ch 6 dsb, p, 6 dsb, sson. R of 3 ds, j to p of previous small r, 5 ds, j to pivotal p of previous large r, 5 ds, p, 3 ds, sson, clr. Ch 6 dsb, p, 6

Fig. 34   Fig. 35   Fig. 36

dsb, sson. Repeat from * twice.

R of 3 ds, j to last p of previous large r, ds, j to first p in first large r, 3 ds, sson, clr. Ch 6 dsb, p, 6 dsb, sson. Run JTN up center of first large r, between strands of cc, and secure cc to base of r. Remove JTN, work in ends and trim (see Figure 36).

Several of these motifs can be combined to make lovely items such as the sachet at the end of this section. The medallion can also be made as a snowflake using JTN #0 and DMC #3 thread.

A Pivotal Picot for Center of Chains: Thread JTN with 3-1/2 yards yarn for cc. Start with left ring of any clover. R of 4 ds, p, 3 ds, p, 2 ds, sson, clr. R of 2 ds, j to last p in previous r, 8 ds, p, 8 ds, p, 2 ds, sson, clr. R of 2 ds, j to last p in previous r, 3 ds, p, 4 ds, sson, clr − first clover completed.

Ch 8 dsb, make a 3/4-inch p when spread open on needle for pivotal picot, 8 dsb, sson. *R of 4 ds, j to last p in previous r of clover, 3 ds, p, 2 ds, sson, clr. R of 2 ds, j to last p in previous r, 8 ds, p, 8 ds, p, 2 ds, sson, clr. R of 2 ds, j to last p in previous r, 3 ds, p, 4 ds, sson, clr. Turn work clockwise, bringing cc toward you, and passing it under ball strand. Pull cc across the previous r, placing JTN next to cc. Ch 8 dsb, j to pivotal p of previous ch, 8 dsb, sson. Turn work counterclockwise, bringing cc to back of work. Repeat from * 3 times.

R of 4 ds, j to last p in previous r, 3 ds, p, 2 ds, sson, clr. R of 2 ds, j to last p in previous r, 8 ds, p, 8 ds, p, 2 ds, sson,

clr. R of 2 ds, j to last p of previous r, 3 ds. Grasp first r of first clover with left hand, bringing it up and around counterclockwise to JTN so that middle large r points to your right hand. J to p in first r of clover (as if to clasp a necklace), 4 ds, sson, clr, making last ch on right side of closed medallion. Ch 8 dsb, j to pivotal p, 8 dsb, sson.

Run JTN up center of first r of first clover, between cc. Secure cc to base of r. Remove JTN, sew in ends and trim (see Figure 37). This medallion makes a lovely snowflake when made with JTN #0 and DMC #3 thread.

MEDALLION AROUND A CENTER RING

A second round has been added to this medallion to illustrate how easily they can be enlarged to be used as coasters or doilies (see Figure 38). Tatting this medallion with a second row and the larger JTN makes nice coasters, or with finer thread and smaller JTN it makes a pretty snowflake. Start by tatting just **one ring** called the **center ring**.

Center Ring: Thread JTN with 24 inches yarn for cc. R of 8 p sep by 2 ds. Ds, p, 2 ds, p, continuing until there are 8 p on JTN and 1 ds on each end, sson, clr. Remove JTN, sew ends into ds on back side of r, two ends one direction, the other two opposite, trim carefully. Right side shows the ridges all around outside edge of r at base of the p. Set aside.

Round (rnd) 1: Thread JTN with 2 yards yarn for cc. R of 4 ds, p, 4 ds, j to

Fig. 37   Fig. 38   Fig. 39

JIFFY NEEDLE TATTING

any p on center r. Be sure the right, or knot side, of ring is facing you. 4 Ds, p, 4 ds, sson, clr. *Ch 4 dsb, p, 5 dsb, p, 4 dsb, sson. R of 4 ds, j to last p of previous r, 4 ds, (avoid twist in joined p in center r), j to next p on left of center r, 4 ds, p, 4 ds, sson, clr. Repeat from * 5 times. Ch 4 dsb, p, 5 dsb, p, 4 dsb, sson. To close rnd, last r as follows: R of 4 ds, j to last p of previous r, 4 ds, j to next p (8th p in center r), 4 ds, j to first p of first r at beginning of rnd, 4 ds, sson, clr. Ch 4 dsb, p, 5 dsb, p, 4 dsb, sson. Run JTN up center of first r, between strands of cc, secure to base of first r. Remove JTN. Thread yarn needle with ends of cc and sew into ds of last ch, sew other ends into first r and trim.

Rnd 2: Thread JTN with 3-1/2 yards yarn for cc. R of 4 ds, p, 4 ds, j to first p of any ch in Rnd 1 (be sure right side is facing you). 4 Ds, p, 4 ds, sson, clr. Ch 11 dsb, sson. *R of 4 ds, j to last p of previous r – avoid twist in connected p. 4 Ds, j to next p on same ch in first rnd, 4 ds, p, 4 ds, sson, clr. Ch 11 dsb, sson. Repeat from * until 13 more rings are completed. R of 4 ds, j to last p of previous r, 4 ds, j to last p in same ch of previous rnd, 4 ds, j to first p of first r at beginning of second rnd, 4 ds, sson, clr.

Ch 11 dsb, sson. Run JTN up center of first r, between strands of cc, and secure to base of r. Remove JTN, work ends of ch in base of first r with a yarn needle as in first rnd (see Figure 38).

SQUARED-OFF MEDALLIONS

Not all medallions can be squared off. Those that can have a multiple of 2 or 4 uniform rings and/or chains. The medallion must have a central design which when squared off will have balance to yield the square. The selected medallion lends itself to be squared off by rings (see Figure 39).

Squared-Off Medallion by Rings: Refer to instructions for *Making a Pivotal Picot for Center of Rings* each time

small r is completed. R of 4 dsb, p, 4 dsb, sson, clr.

The reason this ring is tatted with dsb stitches is because the ring will turn itself around after it is completed. This squared-off medallion could be a snowflake or could be used in strips for insertions, or worked into runners and place mats.

Squared-Off Medallion by Chains: *Medallion with Rings on Inside of Circle* was made with 4 rings on the inside instead of 6 and the chains were elongated as follows: Ch 8 dsb, p, 2 dsb, p, 8 dsb, sson (see Figure 40).

TATTING MEDALLIONS TOGETHER

The First Strip: The medallion in Figure 41 illustrates how to tat medallions together to form a straight line.

Step 1: Tat first medallion from *Medallion with Rings on Inside of Circle* and set aside. Decide whether one or two chains of the first medallion will be joined to one or two chains of the second medallion, since the medallion has 6 chains instead of 8. For practice, two chains of one medallion will be joined to two chains of the other as follows:

Step 2: Second Medallion: Thread JTN with 1-3/4 yards of yarn for cc. R of 5 ds, p, 2 ds, p, 5 ds, sson, clr. Ch 3 dsb, p, 2 dsb, p, 2 dsb. Place medallion in left hand, wrong side of medallion facing – remember the back side has no ridges showing at base of picots. J to middle p of any ch, 2 dsb, p, 2 dsb, p, 3 dsb, sson. Turn work counterclockwise so first medallion hangs below hands. R of 5 ds, j to last p of previous r of second medallion, 2 ds, p, 5 ds, sson, clr.

Turn work clockwise, bringing cc toward you, pulling it down across back of previous r – first medallion is still hanging below second medallion. Ch 3 dsb, p, 2 dsb, p, 2 dsb. Bring up first medallion with left hand, avoiding twist in first p connecting both medallions. J to middle p in next ch to left of first

18

medallion, 2 dsb, p, 2 dsb, p, 3 dsb, sson
– when pulling cc, be sure it remains on
top of work and does not catch on any
other parts. Turn work counterclockwise,
drawing cc to back of work (see Figure
42). Complete a second motif.

Step 3: Repeat Step 2 for next medallion and continue in this manner for
desired length of strip. This strip could
be used as an insertion. Remaining
medallions are joined in the same manner. See left medallion of Figure 43.

Joining a Second Strip to First Strip:
Place first strip on table with one medallion on the left, the other on the right,
right side down.

Step 1: First Medallion of Second
Strip: Thread JTN with 2 yards of yarn
for cc. R of 5 ds, p, 2 ds, p, 5 ds, sson,
clr. Ch 3 ds, p, 2 ds, p, 2 ds, j to middle
p of top ch of first medallion in first strip
(on the left), 2 ds, p, 2 ds, p, 3 ds, sson.
Turn work counterclockwise, allowing
first strip to hang below hands. R of 5
ds, j to last p in first medallion of second strip, 2 ds, p, 5 ds, sson, clr – medallion completed. Place the three joined

medallions on table, right side down.
When completed, they resemble Figure
40; when right side is up, they resemble
Figure 44.

Step 2: Second Medallion of Second
Strip: Place work right side down to
resemble Figure 40. Thread JTN with 2
yards of yarn for cc. R of 5 ds, p, 2 ds,
p, 5 ds, sson, clr. Ch 3 dsb, p, 2 dsb, p,
2 dsb, j to middle p of top ch of second
medallion of first strip (at right), 2 dsb,
p, 2 dsb, p, 3 dsb, sson. Turn work
counterclockwise. R of 5 ds, j to last p
of previous r, 2 ds, p, 5 ds, sson, clr. Turn
work clockwise. Bring cc toward you,
under ball, across previous r. Ch 3 dsb,
p, 2 dsb, p, 2 dsb, j to lower ch of inside
previous medallion (top left in Figure
40).

Bring medallion around to JTN with
left hand. Backside of medallion facing,
j to middle p. 2 Dsb, p, 2 dsb, p, 3 dsb,
sson. Turn work counterclockwise, pulling cc to the back. R of 5 ds, j to last
p of previous r, 2 ds, p, 5 ds, sson, clr.
Turn work clockwise. Bring cc forward
under ball and across previous r. Ch 3

Fig. 40 Fig. 42 Fig. 44

Fig. 41 Fig. 43 Fig. 45

dsb, p, 2 dsb, p, 2 dsb, j to middle p of next ch of previous medallion of second strip. 2 Dsb, p, 2 dsb, p, 3 dsb, sson. Turn work counterclockwise, drawing cc to

PROJECT

Beth's Sachet

This delicate lavender sachet is 3 inches in diameter.

Materials: JTN #00, tapestry needle and threader, scissors, 5 yards DMC #8 pearl cotton, 6x6-inch piece satin, one yard 1/8-inch satin ribbon, lavender potpourri for sachet pouch, matching sewing thread and several straight pins.

Rnd 1: Thread JTN with 1-3/4 yards DMC #8 for cc. R of 4 ds, p, 6 ds, lp (3/4 inch when open on JTN), 6 ds, p, 4 ds, sson, clr. Ch 6 dsb, p, 6 dsb, sson. *R of 4 ds, j to last p of previous r, ds, p, 4 ds, sson, clr. Ch 6 dsb, p, 6 dsb, sson. R of 4 ds, j to last p of previous r, 6 ds, j to middle p of first large r, 6 ds, p, 4 ds, sson, clr. Ch 6 dsb, p, 6 dsb, sson. Repeat from * 3 times. R of 4 ds, j to last p of previous r, ds, j to first p of first r, 4 ds, sson, clr. Ch 6 dsb, p, 6 dsb, sson. Run JTN through center of first r, between strands of cc, and secure on base of r. Remove JTN, sew in ends with tapestry needle.

Rnd 2: Thread JTN with 1-1/4 yards

the back. R of 5 ds, j to last p of previous r, 2 ds, p, 5 ds, sson, clr (see Figure 45 showing right side of medallions).

DMC #8 for cc. Attach cc to middle p of any ch of previous r as follows: With right side facing, run JTN up p, through loop of cc and secure on p. Ch 3 dsb, 3 p sep by 3 dsb, 3 dsb, sson. J to middle p in next ch to the left (avoid twist in first connected p), rnp back between strands of cc and secure on p. Repeat from * 9 times. J to middle p of first ch where first ch is connected. Remove JTN, sew in ends and trim. Repeat Rnds 1 and 2 for other side.

Making Round Pouch for Dry Lavender: Cut a paper circle 3 inches in diameter. Using the paper circle as a pattern, cut two satin circles. Pin circles together, satin (right) sides facing. Pin to hold circles together. With needle and thread take small running back stitches around the circle, leaving a 1-1/2-inch opening. Turn pouch right side out, fill with dry lavender, but do not pack. Turn opening edges in, overcast opening and set aside.

Tatting the Two Panels Together: Thread JTN with 1-1/2 yards DMC #8 for cc. Line up tatted panels right side out. Run JTN through middle p of any ch, first through back panel, then through front panel as if to "sew" edges together. Run JTN through loop of cc, securing cc on p of both panels together. *Ch 3 dsb, 4 p sep by 3 dsb, 3 dsb, sson. Run JTN through middle of p of next ch to left in each panel, between strands of cc, and secure on p. Repeat from * 7 times. Before the next ch are tatted together, stuff round filled pouch into bag. Ch 2 p of last ch tog, remove JTN, sew in ends and trim.

Attaching Ribbon: Cut 12 inches ribbon and tie around one p where outside ch is attached. Leave 2-1/2-inch ends with a 3-inch ribbon loop. Cut 8 inches ribbon for bow over the knot of ribbon loop.

MAKING LONG PICOTS

The instructions in Chapter I explained how fingertip picots are made and used. This chapter describes how long picots are made and used in straight rows and in the rounds of rings and chains, and how long picots can be used in just one ring. Long picots can be made with a single or double ball strand of thread or yarn. Longer single picots are used more often in basic tatting than long double picots; double picots are mainly used in just one ring.

MAKING LONGER SINGLE PICOTS

Long picots can be made in four lengths: one-finger, two-finger, three-finger and four-finger. In Figures 1, 2, 3 and 4, notice how the fingers are holding the JTN and how it lays across the pads of the fingers with the right thumb anchoring the JTN. Fingers are placed next to previous ds on the JTN. Use a

JTN #4 and 4-ply yarn to practice making these picots. The left hand is used to draw strand up across the nails of the fingers and/or back of the fingers and a ds is made next to the index finger on JTN. Remove fingers and slide ds next to previous ds. Pattern will indicate when these long picots are used. Unless otherwise indicated, picots will be fingertip picots — the tiny picot used in traditional tatting.

USING LONG SINGLE PICOTS

Longer single picots may be placed at top and sides of a ring, usually between but sometimes in place of fingertip picots.

"BASKETWEAVE" MOTIF

This motif is composed of two rows. It can also be used to make a basket with DMC #3 and the appropriate JTN.

Thread JTN with 1-1/2 yards of yarn for cc. Only the side picots are elongated and the chains are made a bit longer to compensate for the longer picots between rings.

Row 1: R of 2 ds, 3 one-finger p, 2 ds, p, 2 ds, 3 one-finger p, 2 ds, sson, clr. Ch 5 dsb, p, 5 dsb, sson. *R of 2 ds, j to last lp in previous r, ds, j to next lp in previous r, ds, j to next lp in previous r, 2 ds, p, 3 one-finger p, 2 ds, sson, clr. Ch 5 dsb, p, 5 dsb, sson. Repeat from * for desired length — this row may be started and ended with no picots on the outside edge of the first and last ring.

Row 2: Thread JTN with 1 yard yarn for cc. Place first row in front of you with middle p of r pointing away. Working from right to left, run JTN up center of first r, back through loop of cc, but before securing cc to r, use your thumbs to open middle fingertip p of r and secure cc over open p. *Ch 5 dsb, p, 5 dsb,

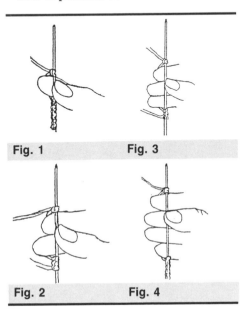

Fig. 1   Fig. 3

Fig. 2   Fig. 4

sson. J to middle p of next r by running JTN up center of next r and back between strands of cc. Open middle p with thumbs and secure cc to open p. Repeat from * for length of first row (see Figure 5).

Another way to join long side picots in the "basketweave" is r of 2 ds, 3 one-finger p, 2 ds, p, 2 ds, 3 one-finger p, 2 ds, sson, clr. *Ch 5 dsb, p, 5 dsb, sson. R of 3 ds, j to last three lp of previous r by sl on JTN, yarn over (ball strand) JTN and pass the 3 p back off over ball strand, forming a stitch on JTN with the loop of the ball strand. Pull ball strand to tighten loop. Ch 3 ds, p, 2 ds, 3 one-finger p, 2 ds, sson, clr. Repeat from * (see Figure 6). Look through shuttle tatting books for additional methods of working rings and chains together.

PROJECTS

Dr. Allen's Little Fir Tree

Begin at the top and work down, noticing that each row gets longer as the tree gets taller. The long picots are worked only into the rings of this pattern.

Materials: JTN #3 or #4 and threader,

The next motif lends itself nicely to longer picots and provides quite an interesting effect. Longer picots are sometimes called "rolling" rings (see Figure 7).

LONGER PICOTS WORKED INTO ROLLING RINGS

Thread JTN with 1-1/2 yards of yarn for cc. *R of 8 ds, p, 2 ds. 5 One-finger p, ending with ds (there will be a r of 8 ds), fingertip p, 2 ds, 5 one-finger p sep by 1 ds, 2 ds, sson, clr. Ch 4 dsb, p, 4 dsb, p, 4 dsb, sson. Run JTN up fingertip p in r, holding ball strand above work (see Figure 8). Run JTN back between two strands of cc. Open p with thumbs, secure to open p by holding other end of r with fingers of left hand. Repeat from *.

yarn needle and scissors, green 4-ply yarn.

Row 1 (Top of Tree): Thread JTN with yarn 3 times length of JTN for cc. R of 4 ds (since this is the top of the tree you may want to work a one-finger p next), 4 ds, p, 2 ds, 5 one-finger p sep by 1 ds, 1 ds, sson, clr. Ch 4 dsb, p, 4 dsb, p, 4 dsb, sson. Join to tp by running JTN up center of r and between strands of cc. Before securing, open p with thumbs and secure ch on open p. Remove JTN, work in ends and trim.

Row 2: Thread JTN with yarn 4 times length of JTN for cc. R of 4 ds, turn top row of tree so side of r with p points up and the right side facing. J to first p on right of the ch to get lp away from work; fold down r. Ch 4 dsb, p, 2 ds, 5 one-finger p sep by 2 ds, 2 ds, sson, clr. Ch 4 dsb, p, 4 dsb, p, 4 dsb, sson. J to tp in r by running JTN up tp in previous r, between strands of cc, and securing on p (rnp); avoid pull on p. R of 4 ds, j to next p in same ch of previous row (tree top), 4 ds, p, 2 ds, 5 one-finger p sep by 2 ds, 2 ds, sson, clr. Ch 4 dsb, p, 4 dsb, p, 4 dsb, sson. J to p in previous r by running JTN up center of r, between strands of cc. Open p with thumbs and secure ch on p.

In this row you j to the p two different ways. The first way is a quick way to join; the second way gives the tree the same finished appearance on the right side as it has on the left side. When joining over p through center of r, special abbreviation rnr (run needle through ring) is used.

Note: The rings of second row in Figure 9 are turned up so you can see how rings of third row are joined to the picot in the chain and the middle ring is bridging two chains. Middle ring in following rows will do the same. Outside rings in each row are joined to only one picot in the previous row.

Row 3: Thread JTN with 1-1/4 yards of yarn for cc. R of 4 ds, j to first p in first ch of previous row, 4 ds, p, 2 ds, 5 one-finger p, 2 ds, sson, clr. Ch 4 dsb, p, 4 dsb, p, 4 dsb, sson. J ch to p in previous r by running JTN up p, between strands of cc, and securing ch to p (rnp). **R of 3 ds, j to last p in same ch of previous row, 2 ds, j to first p in next ch of previous row, 3 ds, p, 2 ds, 5 one-finger p, 2 ds, sson, clr. Ch 4 dsb, p, 4 dsb, p, 4 dsb, sson, j to p of previous r (rnp). **R of 4 ds, j to last p in same ch of previous row, 4 ds, p, 2 ds, 5 one-finger p, 2 ds, sson. Ch 4 dsb, p, 4 dsb, p, 4 dsb, sson. J ch to last p of previous r, rnr. Remove JTN, sew in ends and trim.

Row 4: Repeat Row 3 remembering to repeat pattern between ** once before row is completed.

Row 5: Repeat Row 3 remembering to repeat pattern between ** twice. Rows 6, 7 and 8 each increase by repeating between ** once more each time with each row, lengthening the cc by 4 inches.

Tree Trunk: Thread JTN with 1-1/2 yards yarn for cc. Turn tree upside down, front facing you. Attach cc by running JTN up p between 3rd and 4th r from right, through loop of cc and secure on p. Ch 9 dsb, sson. R of 4 ds, j to last p in ch to left in previous row, 4 ds, p, 4 ds, p, 4 ds, sson, clr. Ch 9 dsb, sson. R of 4 ds, j to last p in previous r, 4 ds, p, 8 ds, sson, clr. Ch 14 dsb, sson. J to last p in previous r by running JTN up p, between strands of cc, and securing on p, ch 14 dsb, sson. R of 8 ds, j to last p in previous r where previous ch and r are connected. Ch 4 ds, p, 4 ds, sson, clr. Ch 9 dsb, sson.

R of 4 ds, j to last p of previous r, 4 ds, j to middle p on opposite side of trunk, 4 ds, j to first p in next ch to left in last row of p, 4 ds, sson, clr. Ch 9 dsb, sson, j to p between 3rd and 4th r of last p from left by running JTN up p, between strands of cc, and securing ch on p. Remove JTN, sew in ends and trim. Beads may be added to "decorate" the tree. Refer to Chapter IV for instructions on working beads into tatting.

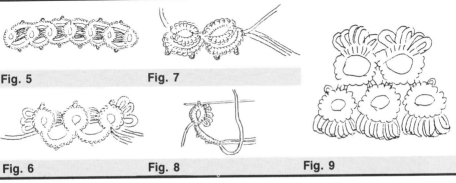

Fig. 5

Fig. 7

Fig. 6

Fig. 8

Fig. 9

23

Small Round Venetian Doily

Small Round Venetian Doily
The long picots are worked into the chains and rings in this doily.

Materials: JTN #3, threader, yarn needle and scissors, 1/4 ounce white, fine 4-ply yarn.

Center Ring: Thread JTN with yarn 3 times length of JTN for cc. R of ds, 8 one-finger p sep by 2 ds, ds, sson, clr. Remove JTN, work in ends and trim.

Rnd 1: Thread JTN with 2-1/2 yards of yarn for cc. R of 3 ds, 1 one-finger p, 3 ds, j to any p in center r. Be sure right side (knot side) is facing. Ch 3 ds, 1 one-finger p, 3 ds, sson, clr. Ch 3 dsb, 8 two-finger p, 3 ds, sson. *R of 3 ds, j to last p of previous r, 3 ds, j to next p in center r to the left (avoid twist in previous connected p), 3 ds, 1 one-finger p, 3 ds, sson, clr. Ch 3 dsb, 8 two-finger p, 3 ds, sson. Repeat from * 5 times. R of 3 ds, j to last p of previous r, 3 ds, j to last p of center r, 3 ds, j to first p in first r at beginning of the rnd, 3 ds, sson, clr. Ch 3 dsb, 8 two-finger p, 3 dsb, sson. Run JTN up center of first r, between strands of cc, and secure to base of first r (rnr). Remove JTN, sew in ends and trim.

Rnd 2: Thread JTN with 2-1/2 yards of yarn for cc. *R of 3 ds, 1 one-finger p, 3 ds, j to last 2 two-finger p in ch of previous rnd and to 2 two-finger p of next ch of previous rnd (4 two-finger p), 3 ds, 1 one-finger p, 3 ds, sson, clr. Ch 3 dsb, 5 one-finger p sep by 2 dsb, 3 dsb, sson. R of 3 ds, j to last p of previous r, 3 ds, j to next 4 two-finger p in same ch of previous rnd, 3 ds, 1 one-finger p, 3 ds, sson, clr. Ch 3 dsb, 5 one-finger p sep by 2 dsb, 3 ds, sson. Repeat from * 7 times, except j first p of each first r to last p of previous r and j to last p of last repeat to the first p of the first r at beginning of the rnd. J last ch to base of first r (rnr).

Run JTN up center of first r at beginning of rnd, between strands of cc, and secure cc to base of r. With yarn needle, sew in ends and trim. Wash according to directions on yarn label.

MAKING PICOT LACE

Picot lace adds a striking touch when used as an insertion with crochet or knit. Picot lace is tatted fringe laced together to form lace. It simulates hairpin lace, but is much more attractive with the rings and chains. There are three types of picot lace strips:

Type 1: No picots on the chains but picots on the rings (see Figure 10). The picots may be three-finger or four-finger picots. Make four-fingered picots with 4-ply yarn, three-finger picots with 3-ply sport weight yarn. These strips are used as edgings.

Sample Strip: Thread JTN #4 with 1-1/2 yards of yarn for cc. R of 3 ds, p, 2 ds, 4 four-finger p, 2 ds, p, 3 ds, sson, clr. *Ch 9 dsb, sson. R of 3 ds, j to last p of previous r, 2 ds, 4 four-finger p, 2 ds, p, 3 ds, sson, clr. Repeat from * for desired length.

Type 2: Picot lace strip is made with picots on rings and chains (see Figure 11). This lace strip is used as center strips. When strips are laced together, they are placed side by side with the chains facing each other and the rings facing each other.

Sample Strip: Thread JTN #4 with 1-1/2 yards of 4-ply yarn for cc. R of 3 ds, p, 2 ds, 4 four-finger p, 2 ds, p, 3 ds, sson, clr. *Ch 3 dsb, 4 four-finger p, 3 dsb. When sson, make sure cc is free of

Fig. 10

Fig. 11

Fig. 12

work, avoiding tangles and not catching other picots as it is pulled through double stitches. R of 3 ds, j to last p of previous r, 2 ds, 4 four-finger p, 2 ds, p, 3 ds, sson, clr. Repeat from * for desired length.

Type 3: This picot lace strip is made with the long picots in the chains only, using middle picots of the rings to join to edgings as fringe or as an insertion when two strips are made and laced together (see Figure 12).

Sample Strip: Thread JTN #4 with 1-1/2 yards of 4-ply yarn for cc.

Row 1: R of 3 ds, p, 3 ds, p (if attaching to knit or crocheted edge, join to the edge here instead of middle picot), 3 ds, p, 3 ds, sson, clr. *Ch 3 dsb, 4 four-finger p, 3 ds, sson. R of 3 ds, j to last p of previous r, 3 ds, p (join here if attaching it to an edge), 3 ds, p, 3 ds, sson, clr. Repeat from * 4 times. Remove JTN, work in ends and trim.

Row 2: Repeat Row 1 to make an insertion.

Lacing Picots Together for Picot Lace: Place strip so the chains with picots are facing each other, right side up (see Figure 12). When using 4-ply yarn, use a size G crochet hook when lacing the picots. Insert hook in first two p of first right lower ch. Catch first 2 p of first left lower ch and pull through right p, leaving left p on hook. Catch next two right p with hook and pull through left p leaving them on hook. Continue in this manner from side to side until all p have been laced together. Thread yarn needle with 5 inches yarn, doubled. Run needle through last 2 p, through loop of folded yarn and secure on p. Fold back p and sew ends of yarn into ch and r to secure p.

To make a stole, place lace strips side by side with rings of one strip facing the rings of other strip; the p in the ch face each other. Lace Type 1 is used for outside edge, giving a finished appearance. When a more open effect is desired, four loops of fringe are laced together at once.

PROJECT

Cathy's Little Picot Lace Hat

This hat is made of Type 2 picot lace. The band is knit ribbing and a picot rose forms the pompon.

Materials: JTN #3 and threader, yarn needle and scissors, size G crochet hook, size 7 double-pointed knitting needles, 2 ounces 4-ply yarn and a safety pin for marker.

Step 1 – Body of Hat: Thread JTN with 1-1/2 yards of yarn for cc. R of 3 ds, p, 2 ds, 4 four-finger p, 2 ds, p, 3 ds, sson, clr. *Ch 3 dsb, 4 four-finger p, 3 dsb, sson. R of 3 ds, j to last p of previous r, 2 ds, 4 four-finger p, 2 ds, p, 3 ds, sson, clr (when sson, be sure to straighten cc to avoid catching the p). Repeat from * 4 times – 6 r. Remove JTN, sew in ends and trim. Set aside the first strip. Repeat Step 1 seven times.

Step 2 – Assembling the Strips: Place strips vertically, right side up with ch on inside. Place a third strip vertically to the right of first two strips right side up, rings to rings; lace picots. Repeat Step 2 until all strips are laced together. To ease the lacing of last side of 8th strip

to first strip, it helps to slip a book or magazine through the body of the hat.

Step 3 – Ribbing For Hat: Using size G crochet hook and yarn, turn hat upside down so tied loop ends are down. Join yarn to side tp of r to the right of any lacing by spreading apart p with thumbs and sc over open p. Ch 3, working from right to left, *catch 4 sides of first two p at left of r with sc, ch 2, sc over sides of next two p to the left, but on the right of next r, ch 3.

Repeat from * moving to next r at left until all ends of strips have been crocheted into the rnd. Sl st into first sc at beginning of rnd. Do not cut yarn. Pick up a st in each ch and sc around hat, placing each st on knitting needles evenly divided (26,26,27) – 79 sts. Place marker or pin.

One st at beginning of rnd – 80 sts. Work in k 2, p 2 for 1-1/2 inches. Bind off, work in ends and trim.

Step 4 – Crown:

Rnd 1: Join yarn with crochet hook to side p of any r at top of hat. *Ch 1, work from right to left. Sc over sides of double p. Ch 1, sc in sides of left two top double p, ch 1, sc in p of next r. Repeat from * around crown. Sl st in sc of p at first r. Do not cut yarn.

Rnd 2: Ch 2, *insert hook in next st and hold it on hook. Insert hook in next st, yarn over, pull loop through all 3 sts on hook. Repeat from * around crown. Sl st in top st of ch, ch 2. Repeat from * once, closing crown. Cut yarn and pull end through. Set aside.

Step 5 – Picot Rose: Make picot fringe by threading JTN with 1 yard of yarn for cc. Measure 4-1/2 yards of yarn from skein. Do not cut; fold yarn at that point, interlocking loop of ball strand with loop of cc by running JTN through loop of ball strand and loop of cc and securing loops. Pull apart to lock loops together. Place interlocked loops under thumb, ch 1 ds next to interlocked loops. Ch 8 three-finger double p, 1 double fingertip p. *2 Three-finger double p, 1 fingertip double p. Repeat from * 3 times. 4 Three-finger double p, 1 one-finger double p, 1 fingertip double p, sson. Do not cut ball strand.

Use ball strand to crochet back across tips of p, beginning at fingertip double p at right end of fringe. Ch 1, *sc in back of next double p, ch 1, sc in front of same double p, ch 1. Repeat from * across top of each individual p to next fingertip p. Ch 3, sc in fingertip double p together, ch 3. Continue in this manner across top

of lp and in the creases, ending with ch 4 and sc into ds at end of fringe. Remove hook, work in end and trim.

Shape rose and attach to crown of hat. Pull cc end at right end of fringe (knot side faces you). Pull cc to right end of fringe and gather p. Thread yarn needle with a single strand and let it hang. Grasp all ends next to first ds with right thumb and index finger, wrap fringe around clockwise as tight as possible in a spiral. Place rose face down and with threaded yarn needle sew through ds in crisscross fashion to secure spiral. Push ends through tiny hole in crown and sew rose to hat. Tie two ends together, trimming about 1-1/2 inches from base of rose.

MAKING LONG DOUBLE PICOTS IN ONE RING

Picots used in just one ring become daisies. Double picot daisies are used more often than single picot daisies because they have a fuller appearance, are stronger and can stand more wear and tear than single picot daisies. These daisies, by changing number of fingers used in making the double picots, can produce trims such as butterflies, hearts and stars. There are occasions when single picot daisies are used and then only one ball strand is used.

MAKING THE DOUBLE PICOT DAISY

The double picot is made the same as long picots except in making double picots, the ball strand must be doubled.

Step 1: Thread JTN with 24 inches of yarn for cc.

Step 2: Measure 4 yards of yarn, double, then cut. Do this for all Lark's Head Knots. With loop end attach the JTN with a Lark's Head Knot by folding loop over JTN toward you. Hold folded loop with left hand, pull JTN out of fold and weave it back through the two loops made by the fold and secure it on the JTN (see Figure 13).

Step 3: Grasp JTN in front of ds (Lark's Head Knot), make three-finger double picot daisy with the double ball strand (see Figures 14 and 15). Make 16

Fig. 13

Fig. 14

Fig. 15

double picots, sson, clr. Cradle JTN with all the stitches in the left hand. Separate and straighten cc hanging from the work in the left hand, preventing cc from catching in work.

With right hand grasp front end of JTN and pull up to slide stitches onto cc (see Figure 16), sson, clr (see Figure 17). Remove JTN and turn daisy over.

With yarn needle work in ends – two one direction and two the opposite around ring and trim (see Figure 18). These daisy figures can be combined with crochet or tatted together to make many projects. The following designs are practice projects for making double picots using a different number of picots.

PROJECTS

Five Pointed Daisy Star

Materials: JTN #2 and threader, yarn needle, size G crochet hook, 8 yards white sport weight yarn with glitter.

Step 1: Thread JTN with 24 inches yarn for cc. Cut and double 4 yards of yarn, attach to JTN with a Lark's Head Knot. R of 3 three-finger dp, *fingertip dp, 3 three-finger dp. Repeat from * 3 times, sson, clr. With yarn needle, sew in ends and trim.

Step 2: With size G crochet hook and yarn, join yarn to any fingertip dp in star with sc. *Ch 5, sc in 3 three-finger dp to the left (right side of star facing), ch 2, sc back in same 3 dp to form point, ch 5, sc in next fingertip dp. Ch 5, sc in next 3 three-finger dp, ch 2, sc in same place. Repeat from * 3 times, ending with ch 6 and pulling end through last ch. Using needle, stitch into next fingertip dp at beginning of rnd and trim. Attach ties to one of the points. **Note:** A 6-pointed star is made by repeating 4 times when making the 3 three-finger dp.

Fig. 16

Fig. 17

Fig. 18

Daisy Heart

Materials: JTN #2 and threader, yarn needle, size G crochet hook, scissors, 4-3/4 yards red sport weight yarn, 2 yards contrasting color white or gold metallic yarn.

Step 1: Thread JTN with 24 inches red yarn for cc. Fold remaining red yarn in half and attach to JTN with a Lark's Head Knot. R of 1 one-finger dp, 3 three-finger dp, 1 two-finger dp, 1 one-finger dp, 1 two-finger dp, 1 three-finger dp, 1 two-finger dp, 1 one-finger dp, 1 two-finger dp, 3 three-finger dp, 1 one-finger dp, sson, clr. With yarn needle, sew in ends and trim.

Step 2: With crochet hook and contrasting yarn, join yarn to crease of heart or base of r with sc. Ch 2, sc in dp at left (right side of heart facing). Ch 2, sc in next dp, ch 1, sc in next dp. Repeat around to long dp in point of heart, sc in dp, 2 ch, sc.

*Sc in next dp up other side of heart, ch 1. Repeat from * to within last 2 dp, ending with sc in next dp, ch 2, sc in last dp, ch 3 and pull yarn through last ch. With yarn needle make several small overhand sts with the ends in crease of heart and leave the ends for ties.

The Marigold Motif

This motif is edged with tatted rings and chains.

Materials: JTN #3 and threader, 1/2 ounce gold 4-ply yarn, yarn needle and scissors.

Step 1: Make 12 two-finger double picot daisies, sson, clr. Remove JTN, work in ends and trim.

Step 2: Thread JTN with 3 yards yarn for cc. R of 3 ds, p, 3 ds, j to any double p in daisy (be sure knot side of daisy is facing — right side), 3 ds, p, 3 ds, sson, clr. Ch 4 dsb, p, 4 dsb, sson. *R of 3 ds, j to last p of previous r, 3 ds, j to next double p in daisy, 3 ds, p, 3 ds, sson, clr. Ch 4 dsb, p, 4 dsb, sson. Repeat from * 9 times. R of 3 ds, j to last p of previous r, 3 ds, j to last double p of the daisy, 3 ds, j to first p of first r, 3 ds, sson, clr. Ch 4 dsb, p, 4 dsb, sson. Run JTN through base of first r, between strands of cc, and secure to base of first r. Remove JTN, sew in ends with yarn needle and trim.

EXTENDED LONGER DOUBLE PICOTS

The *extended* long double picots are longer than long double picots and are used to make tassels. There is only one ring.

Step 1: Thread JTN with 30 inches yarn for cc.

Step 2: Measure 7 yards yarn, double and attach to JTN with a Lark's Head Knot.

Step 3: Grasp JTN across the index and three fingers of right hand in front of the Lark's Head Knot. With left hand wrap double ball strand around all the fingers by drawing double ball strand across back of four fingers, around outside edge of index finger, down across inside of all the fingers, around outside edge of little finger, back across back of the fingers again and tat 1 ds (see Figure 19). Remove fingers and slide ds next to previous ds (Lark's Head). Repeat Step 3 until 12 extended long double picots have been made, sson, clr. Do not cut cc and do not remove JTN. Work in other two ends of ball strand and trim.

Shaping Tassel: Place end of right index finger under center of r, smoothing all extended long picots around it (see Figure 20). With tassel in left hand and JTN and cc in right hand, wrap cc around the rim 3/4 inch from ds of tassel in a counterclockwise direction once and insert JTN into loop of the cc (see Figure 21).

Remove finger and pull JTN and cc through loop of cc to tighten tassel; wrap cc around three or four more times, ending by inserting the tip of JTN into tassel just below the wrapped yarn and working it up through center of r at top of tassel. Pull JTN with cc through to be used as ties (see Figure 22). For a fuller tassel, allow a longer ball or skein strand and tat more extended long picots.

PROJECT

Angel Daisy Tassel Ornament

Materials: JTN #3 or 4 and JTN #0, threader, scissors, yarn needle, 15 yards 4-ply white yarn, 6-inch strand red 4-ply yarn, 30 yards gold metallic thread, a 6-1/2-inch white chenille stem, a 22mm wooden bead for head, nine 6mm gold beads, 8-inch piece fine wire to string beads.

Step 1 — Body Tassel: Thread JTN #3 or #4 with 1-1/2 yards of white 4-ply yarn for cc. Make as many extended long dp as ball strand allows.

Step 2 — Making the Arms: Run chenille stem through top part of tassel between the gathered waist and shoulders. When in place, insert end of right arm

| Fig. 19 | Fig. 20 | Fig. 21 | Fig. 22 | Fig. 23 |

in eye of JTN and fold end back 1/4 inch. With white yarn, leaving a 6-inch end, tat *2 dsb, p, repeat from * 6 times, ending with 5 dsb, sson on chenille stem. Distribute stitches evenly, remove JTN, leaving a 6-inch end. Fold back last 2 dsb, with yarn needle make 2 or 3 sts in figure "8" over folded end to form "hand." Leave yarn end hanging from hand. Insert end of left arm in JTN. With 4-ply white yarn, tat *2 ds, p, repeat from * 6 times. Remove JTN and finish left hand as before. Leave yarn ends at hands and shoulders hanging.

Step 3 – Attaching Head: Thread shoulder ends from arms with yarn needle one at a time, inserting needle in "shoulders" up through center of wooden bead. There should be 4 yarn ends coming through bead head. Divide ends in half and tie together in a knot at top of head, running 2 of the ends down through bead head and body; remaining ends are used as ties.

Step 4 – Making Wings: Thread JTN #0 with 2-1/2 yards of metallic thread for cc. DMC #3 gold thread can be used for cc if desired.

Center Ring for Wings: R of 2 ds, 9 p sep by 2 ds, 2 ds, sson, clr. **Ch 12 dsb, sson. R of 8 ds, j to first p in r to the right of ch (the end of r is at left), 3 ds,

p, 5 ds, sson, clr. *Ch 3 ds, 5 p sep by 2 ds, 3 ds, sson. R of 5 ds, j to last p in previous r, 3 ds, j to next p in center r, 3 ds, p, 5 ds, sson, clr. Repeat from * once.

Ch 3 ds, 5 p sep by 2 ds, 3 ds, sson. R of 5 ds, j to last p of previous r, 3 ds, j to next p in center r, 8 ds, sson, clr. Ch 12 dsb, sson. J ch to next p in center r by running JTN up p between strands of cc and securing ch on p – avoid pulling p (see Figure 23). Do not cut cc – one wing complete. Repeat from ** for the other wing. J last ch to base of center r by running JTN up center of r, between strands of cc, and securing ch to base of r. Remove JTN, sew in ends and trim. Attach to back of shoulders with gold metallic thread.

Step 5 – Making Halo: Thread JTN #0 with 18 inches thread for cc. Ch ds, 8 p sep by 2 ds, ds, sson, clr. Sew in 3 ends and let the 4th hang. Run white ends at top of head through center of halo with yarn needle (knot side of halo up). With 4th gold end from halo, tack halo to knot on top of head and back into halo, trim carefully.

Step 6 – Making Wreath: With fine wire, string 9 gold beads on 4-ply yarn, tie beads in a circle. Attach wreath to hands with remaining yarn on hands, sew ends back into each arm and trim.

INCREASING AND DECREASING, ADDITIONAL STITCHES AND PICOTS

This chapter includes instructions on manipulating double stitches to make interesting textured stitches, decreasing and increasing in tatting, making a measured picot, and making twin picots.

SPECIAL TECHNIQUES MANIPULATING PART OR ALL OF THE DOUBLE STITCHES

Before proceeding with the special techniques, let's look at the regular tatted double stitch from a different perspective. Figure 1 shows 10 regular tatted double stitches on the JTN. When the double stitches on the JTN are turned to the right side, the bottom edge of the double stitch resembles Figure 2.

Notice two rows of "ridges" running side by side to form the row of double stitches. The "ridges" of the top row are referred to as upper loops and those of the bottom row are lower loops. In the special techniques of this chapter, these "ridges" or "loops" will be manipulated to achieve particular effects. They are manipulated by using only the first half hitch (fhh), or the second half hitch (shh), of the double stitch at a time. The following techniques are variations of this manipulation.

RIGHT TWIST STITCH

The right twist is made by making only the fhh (the first half hitch on the JTN which involves the upper ridges of the double stitches). To make a handle on a small tatted basket, thread JTN #0 with double strand of DMC #3 for desired length of handle. Attach looped end to one point on top edge of basket, usually a ring, by running JTN through top ring and then through loop of cc. Secure on r. Tat only fhh on the JTN. Fill JTN with fhh and ease them slowly onto cc, continuing to make fhh on JTN until cc is covered. As fhh are made, the chain will twist to the right. As it twists, it will be necessary to turn the JTN as work progresses to accommodate the twisting taking place (see Figure 3).

LEFT TWIST STITCH

This stitch is made by tatting only shh on the JTN (see Figure 4). The shh seems easier to make because it's not likely that you'll slip into making the other half of the ds when only half hitches are desired.

JOSEPHINE KNOT

Many shuttle tatting books refer to the Josephine Knot as a picot or knot. Actually it is a tiny ring that is used in

Fig. 1

Fig. 3

Fig. 2

Fig. 4

place of a picot. With a shuttle it is made with fine thread, so it is understandable why it was referred to as a picot or knot. It is made by tatting only the fhh or the shh of the ds. It is placed on chains in place of a picot and that is why it is referred to as a picot. The following example explains how it is made on chains of an edging of rings and chains:

*R of 3 ds, 3 p sep by 3 ds, 3 ds, sson, clr. Ch 4 dsb, sson. 9 Shh the Josephine

Knot (jk), sson, clr. After r is closed, grasp and hold it between thumb and index finger of left hand. Grasp cc close to jk with right thumb and index finger and pull cc down toward left hand in a clockwise direction to tighten the ring or Josephine Knot. Ch 4 dsb, sson. R of 3 ds, j to last p in previous r, 3 ds, p, 3 ds, p, 3 ds, sson, clr. Repeat from *. This edging can be used to trim a handkerchief.

PROJECT

Josie's Handkerchief with Josephine Knot Trim

The tatted edging for this handkerchief is basically all chains. It is a practice project for making Josephine Knots.

Materials: JTN #000 and threader, scissors and an embroidery needle, 1/4 ball white DMC #8 pearl cotton, 12 yards white DMC #12 pearl cotton, 12 yards rose DMC #8 pearl cotton, hemstitched white handkerchief.

Row 1 – White Chains:

Step 1: Thread JTN with 2 yards

DMC #12 for cc, *attach cc to hem space at left of any handkerchief corner by running JTN through hem space back through loop of cc and securing cc to corner. With white DMC #8, ch 8 dsb, sson. Fit tatted ch around corner of handkerchief and j to first hem space on right side of same corner by running JTN through space, between strands of cc, and securing to edge.

Step 2: **Ch 8 dsb, sson. Count 4 hem spaces to the right and j in the 4th space by running JTN through it and between strands of cc, secure in place. Repeat from ** to second corner. Repeat Step 1 from *. Repeat Step 2 for next side. Repeat Step 1 for third corner. Repeat Step 2 for next side. Repeat Step 1 for fourth corner. Repeat Step 2 for last side, ending in same hem space where chaining started. Remove JTN, sew in ends and trim.

Row 2 – Rose Josephine Knot and Chain Trim: This trim runs parallel to previous white chain. The jk is made on every other rose chain.

Step 1: Thread JTN with 2 yards white DMC #12 for cc. Count 15 white ch to the left from any corner – do not count corner ch. Attach cc to handkerchief edge over same attachment made in previous ch by running JTN through same hem space on left of 5th ch, back through loop of cc, and securing to edge between the two white ch. **Working with rose color, ch 12 dsb, sson — plain rose chain.

Attach ch to same right hem space of same ch of previous row by running JTN through same space, between strands of cc, and securing to edge of handkerchief between next two white ch. Ch 8 dsb, sson. 10 Shh for jk, sson, clr. Ch 8 dsb, sson. Attach to same hem space between next two white chains of previous row — first Josephine point complete. Repeat from ** 14 times over every white ch of previous row including the corner, ending with plain rose ch of 12 dsb, sson. Attach to handkerchief, remove JTN

and work in ends.

Step 2 – Rose Appliqué: Thread JTN with 2 yards white DMC #12 for cc. With rose thread, r of 5 ds, p, 2 ds, p, 5 ds, sson, clr. Ch 8 dsb, sson. 10 Shh for jk, sson, clr. Ch 8 dsb, sson. R of 5 ds, j to last p of previous r, 2 ds, p, 5 ds, sson, clr. Ch 8 dsb, sson. 10 Shh for jk, sson, clr. Ch 8 dsb, sson.

Repeat from * (Row 1) 3 times, r of 5 ds, j to last p of previous r, 2 ds, j to first p of first r, 5 ds, sson, clr. Ch 8 dsb, sson. 10 Shh for jk, sson, clr. Ch 8 dsb, sson. Run JTN through center of first r, between strands of cc, and secure to base of first r. Do not cut cc. Pin medallion to corner of handkerchief bounded by Josephine points. Stitch to handkerchief with ends of white cc, trim and steam press.

NODE STITCH

The node stitch is sometimes called the ric-rac or zig-zag stitch. When it is made, an equal number of fhh and shh are alternated to form the nodes. To practice, tat ds, *3 fhh followed by 3 shh. Repeat from * 3 times, ending with 2 ds (see Figure 5). Remember the node stitch must always have an equal number of fhh and shh to produce the ric-rac effect. The fhh raised the stitches and the shh lowered the stitches. The node stitch can be used between the picot in rings and chains. They are used when a more textured appearance is desired and are often used in tatted pictures of flowers or on church linens and vestments.

ROLLED STITCH

The rolled stitch is used to remove some of the texture made by the ridges of regular tatting, particularly if a smooth effect is desired. Make the rolled stitch in a ring. R of 1 ds, wrap ball strand around JTN tightly 5 times (five rolls), ds, p, ds, wrap 5 rolls, ds, p, ds, wrap 5 rolls, ds, p, ds, wrap 5 rolls, ds (see Figure 6), sson, clr. Do the same for chains to remove texture.

This stitch must be wrapped tightly and the ball strand held taut when wrapping. The rolls are held in place by the ds tatted at each end of each wrapped segment. The roll can have more wraps if a longer smooth cord is desired. These stitches work best when made on threads that have some friction such as cotton, linen or silk. The use of rayon is not recommended. Synthetic threads that provide some friction can be used. Remember a ds must be placed at each end of each wrapped segment to hold wraps in place.

Fig. 5

Fig. 6

PADDED TATTING

For padded tatting, simply use a heavier thread or yarn for cc and a finer thread or yarn for ball strand. This gives the effect of a "ballooned" ring and chain with finer tatted ridges around the rings and chains. Striking effects can be achieved by using different types of yarns together.

PROJECT

Minnie's Puffed Hot Pad

This is a padded doily worked with white J & P Coats Speed Cro-Sheen crochet thread over Aunt Lydia's white rug yarn. It is called a puff doily or hot pad because it uses two different thread/yarn weights, the rings and chains balloon a bit and the ridges are finer around the edges of the rings and chains.

Materials: JTN #5 and threader, yarn needle and scissors, 1/2 ball of J & P Coats Speed Cro-Sheen crochet thread in desired color, 12 yards rug yarn to match crochet thread.

Rnd 1 – Center Round: Thread JTN with 1-3/4 yards rug yarn for cc. R of 4 ds, p, 4 ds, 3/4-inch p when open on JTN – this is a pivotal picot, 4 ds, p, 4 ds, sson, clr. Ch 3 dsb, 3 p sep by 4 dsb, 3 dsb, sson. *R of 4 ds, j to last p in previous r, 4 ds, j to middle p of first r, 4

ds, p, 4 ds, sson, clr. Ch 3 dsb, p, 3 p sep by 4 dsb, 3 dsb, sson. Repeat from * 3 times. R of 4 ds, j to last p of previous r, 4 ds, j to middle p of first r, 4 ds, j to first p in first r at beginning of r, 4 ds, sson, clr. Ch 3 dsb, 3 p sep by 4 dsb, 3 dsb, sson. Run JTN up center of first r, between strands of cc, and secure to base of r. Remove JTN, sew in ends and trim.

Rnd 2: Thread JTN with 1-3/4 yards rug yarn for cc. *R of 6 ds, j to last p in any ch of previous rnd, ds, j to first p in next ch of previous rnd, 6 ds, sson, clr. Ch 3 dsb, p, 6 dsb, p, 3 dsb, sson. J to middle p of same ch of previous rnd by running JTN up p, cc and secure on p (avoid pull on p). Turn work clockwise, bringing cc toward you under ball strand. Pull cc across top of previous ch in rnd. Ch 3 dsb, j to last p in ch at left, 6 dsb, p, 3 dsb, sson. Turn work counterclockwise and pull cc to back of work. Repeat from * of previous rnd 5 times. Run JTN up center of first r, between strands of cc, and secure to base of r. Remove JTN, work in ends and trim.

Rnd 3: Thread JTN with 2-1/4 yards rug yarn for cc. *R of 3 ds, p, 3 ds, j to middle p of right ch of previous rnd, 3 ds, p, 3 ds, sson, clr. Ch 12 dsb, sson. R of 3 ds, j to last p of previous r, 6 ds, j to p at two ch of previous rnd, 6 ds, p, 3 ds, sson, clr. Ch 12 dsb, sson. R of 3 ds, j to last p in previous r, 3 ds, j to p at left ch of previous rnd, 3 ds, p, 3 ds, sson, clr (first group of rings complete). Ch 12 dsb, sson. Repeat from * 5 times, but in each first r of group, j to last p in last r of previous group. At last p of last r of last group, j to first p in first r of first group. Ch 3 ds, sson, clr, ending with 12 dsb, sson. Run JTN up center of r, between strands of cc, and

secure on base of r. Remove JTN, work in ends and trim.

This padded doily can also be made with JTN #4 using 4-ply yarn for cc and same color baby yarn for the ball strand.

SOLID CHAINING SPIRAL STITCH

For a solid effect, chain is worked in a spiral. Use a JTN #4 or #5 and either worsted weight or rug yarn. Thread JTN with 2 yards of yarn for cc. R of 3 ds, 3

tp sep by 3 ds, 3 ds, sson, clr. Leave a space between r and ch. *Ch 5 ds (the dsb sts are not used because a better spiral is made by tatting chain clockwise).

PROJECT

Mesa Hot Pad

This hot pad made of rug yarn simulates reed and raffia work. The center begins with a ring and is completed with chains. To get the spiral effect, work from left to right in a clockwise direction to ensure a smooth transition from ring to chain. Because chains are made clockwise, double stitches are ds, not dsb. With this method two different kinds of tiny picots are used to make the spiral explained in this pattern.

Materials: JTN #5 and threader, yarn needle and scissors, white and red rug yarn.

Center Disk of Hot Pad: Thread JTN with 2 yards of yarn for cc.

Rnd 1: (**Note:** A tp is made between the ch and the r by spacing the ds a bit from the r). Work in the tail of ball strand before making tp. Grasp JTN as if to make a ch, place the tip of the right thumb partly on the base of r and partly on JTN before making ch. Anchor JTN under thumb and r with right index finger. By placing the tip of the right thumb this way before making the ds, it will ensure a "space between the ch and ring." Ch 5 ds, sson (see Figure 7). Notice yarn between r and ds on JTN. When ds are sson, the short intervening strand forms a tiny picot, called a spaced picot (sp p).

Continue with spiral, sson ds on JTN and run JTN up first p to the right in the r, between strands of cc, and secure ch to p (see Figure 8). Spaced picot (sp p), 5 ds, sson. J to next p in r. Sp p, 5 ds, sson. J to 3rd p in r. Sp p, 5 ds, j to first sp (first p at beginning of rnd).

Rnd 2: *Sp p, 3 ds, p (index fingertip p), 3 ds, sson, j to next p. Repeat from * around.

Rnd 3: *Sp p, 5 ds, sson, j to next p. Repeat from * around.

Rnd 4: Cut white yarn 2-1/2 inches from work. With red, 5 ds, sson. J to next p. Work in ends — white ends into red ch, trim; red end into white ch, trim. When working in these ends leave a tp at this point with yarn needle to mark beginning of rnd. It also serves as first sp p for beginning of next rnd. *Sp p, 5 ds, sson, j to next p. Repeat from * around to color change, j last ch of rnd at that point.

Rnd 5: *Sp p, 4 ds, sson, j to next p. Repeat from *. Cut red.

Rnd 6: Ch 5 ds, j to next p, sson. Work in ends as before, leaving a tp with one of the ends. *Sp p, 5 ds, sson, j to next p. Repeat from * around to color change. Remove JTN and work in ends.

Red Border: Thread JTN with 2-1/2 yards of yarn for cc. R of 3 ds, p, 3 ds, j to any p on rnd (be sure right side is facing), 3 ds, p, 3 ds, sson. Ch 10 dsb, sson. *R of 3 ds, j to last p in previous r, 3 ds, j to next p, 3 ds, p, 3 ds, sson, clr. Ch 10 dsb, sson. Repeat from * around to last tp on rnd — 17 r. R of 3 ds, j to last p of previous r, 3 ds, j to last tp, 3 ds, j to first p in first r in rnd, 3 ds, sson, clr. Ch 10 dsb, sson. Run JTN up center of first r, between strands of cc, and secure ch to base of r. Remove JTN, work in ends and trim.

THE RUNNING STITCH

The running stitch is simply a chain of regular dsb which are stretched out as far as possible after being taken off the JTN. This chain can be a necklace or cord (see Figure 9).

PARALLEL TATTING

Parallel tatting is a unique cord made on two sides of the JTN at the same time. This cord is then used as a base to add beads, picots and other tatting.

To Parallel Tat: Thread JTN with 1 yard of 4-ply yarn for cc. Measure 4 yards from ball and double it; do not cut. Hold ball strand loop in left hand, run JTN through ball strand loop, through loop of cc, and secure the loops together by pulling them "apart" to interlock them. Place interlocked loops under right thumb against JTN. Drape one of the ball strands along right thumb, other ball strand over fingers of right hand and let it hang down the right side

— cc hangs down through the hand (see Figure 10) holding JTN up straight and pointing up.

*With left hand pick up left strand hanging down right thumb and tat a ds next to interlocked loops under right thumb. Drop strand and bend wrist towards you. With left hand pick up right strand off right hand and tat 1 dsb next to previous ds on JTN. Drop right strand back on right hand and release right wrist. Repeat from * three times.

Keeping strands separated, tat 1 one-finger p on left with left strand and then 1 one-finger p on right with right strand. Dsb on left and dsb on right, alternating twice. Make a single one-finger p on each side, followed by 6 dsb and 6 dsb alternately (see Figure 11). Ball strands of parallel tatting can be strung with beads. In place of picots, push beads up to JTN between the ds. Chapter IV shows methods of working beads with parallel tatting.

| Fig. 7 | Fig. 8 | Fig. 9 | Fig. 10 | Fig. 11 |

PROJECT

The Picot Tree

Ball strand of parallel tatting can be doubled and worked as the picot tree. Thread JTN #4 or #5 with 30 inches of 4-ply yarn for cc. Cut two 3-3/4-yard lengths of 4-ply yarn, doubling both strands. Interlock the two loops by running JTN through two loops of the double ball strands, through loop of cc, and securing them "apart" to lock together. Position right hand and double strands as shown in Figure 10.

Ds with left double strand and dsb with right double strand alternately on JTN 5 times. Tat 1 four-finger dp alternately for first two lower limbs of tree twice. Tat 1 three-finger dp alternately for next two limbs twice. Tat 1 two-finger p alternately for next limbs alternately twice. Tat 1 one-finger dp alternately, 1 fingertip p alternately once for top limbs, ending ds, dsb to complete top of tree (see Figure 12). Sson on cc all the way down to interlocked loops, avoid bunching knots. Remove JTN, threading two ends of cc with a yarn needle.

Skip top ds (otherwise it will unravel) sewing ends back into parallel ds to secure the tree. Work one ball strand from each side back into tree; remaining two strands are for ties. Beads and sequins can be strung on ball strands before beginning ds. To complete the decoration, sew a gold thread garland fashion across tree.

Parallel Tatting Can Also Be Turned into Running Stitches: To make them "run," repeat *To Parallel Tat* , after sts are sson, stretch them out on cc (see Figure 13). This running st is used on parts of necklaces. See Chapter IV for methods of working beads into this cord.

MAKING DECREASES AND INCREASES IN TATTING

DECREASES

A decrease is achieved by tatting a ring and joining it to a chain of previous row, immediately making another ring and joining it to next chain (see Figure 14).

INCREASES

The simplest way to increase is to join two rings in the same chain of previous row (see Figure 15).

Other ways to decrease and increase include making larger or smaller rings, longer or shorter chains. Knowing how to decrease and increase will help in planning new patterns.

MEASURED PICOT

To make a measured picot (mp) use a piece of cardboard cut to a specific size. The cardboard is substituted for the fingers when all the picots are exactly the same. Measured picots (mp) are used when several people plan to work on the same project. Place desired length cardboard under the JTN next to previous ds or dsb on JTN. Draw ball strand up across back of cardboard and make ds or dsb instructed in pattern (see Figure 16). Remove cardboard, slide ds next to previous ds on JTN.

MAKING TWIN PICOTS

Twin picots are 2 fingertip picots made one right after the other wherever twin fingertip picots are placed on the ring or chain. They give added strength when fine yarn is used for an article and may get some wear and tear.

Ring of Twin Picots: Ch 3 ds, twin picots, 3 ds, twin picots, 3 ds, twin picots, 3 ds, sson, clr (see Figure 17).

MAKING A MOCK RING

The mock ring is a chain where the two ends join to become one picot. Practice by tatting a daisy: R of 2 ds, 7 p sep by 2 ds, 2 ds, sson, clr. Ch 6 ds, p, 6 ds, sson. Run JTN up center of r, between strands of cc, and secure ch to base of r. With right side facing, work around r clockwise and *run JTN through p to the right from back to front, so it is in position for next petal. Ch 6 ds, p, 6 ds, sson. Run JTN through strands of cc and secure petal to p. Repeat from * — with this r, there are no ch between the r's.

JOINING THE TATTED CHAIN TO BASE OF RING IN ONE MOTION

JTN is inserted through center of a r from back of work; JTN tip is under ball strand and between strands of cc. Pull JTN up, bringing cc through the r; ch can then be secured to base of r. The abbreviation for this procedure is rnr (run needle through ring) to base of r (see Figure 18).

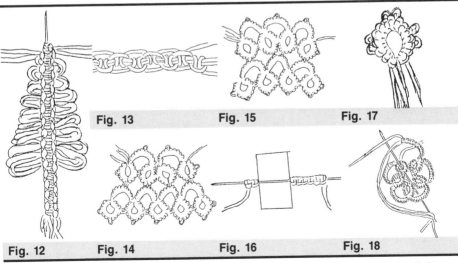

Fig. 13   Fig. 15   Fig. 17

Fig. 12   Fig. 14   Fig. 16   Fig. 18

COMBINING JIFFY NEEDLE TATTING WITH BEADS

Elegant collars, belts, jewelry and decorations result when a creative imagination combines beads with tatting.

TYPES AND SIZES OF BEADS TO USE

SUGGESTED BEAD SIZES TO USE WITH DIFFERENT JIFFY TATTING NEEDLES

JTN	BEADS
0000	2mm, 2.5mm
000	Up to 3.0mm
00	Up to 4.0mm
0-2	Between 3mm and 6mm
3-5	Between 4mm and 8mm

Oval and teardrop shapes can be used with any size JTN; remember, however, to select the smaller ones when using finer tatting needles, the larger beads with the larger tatting needles. Purchasing beads in quantity is suggested for economy and for color consistency. Start with patterns using only a few beads to learn the techniques in working beads into various tatting projects.

COMBINING BEADS WITH TATTING

Normally beads are worked into rings

Fig. 1

Fig. 2

and chains between double stitches. They can also be threaded on picots individually, placed in position in the center of a ring, at the base of a ring or threaded on the carrying cord.

STRINGING BEADS ON BALL STRAND

The four ways to string beads are:
(1) Fold a 6-inch piece of fine wire to use as a needle and thread with end of the ball strand (see Figure 1).
(2) To combine larger beads with tatting, use beads with large holes. To string these beads, use a size 0 or 1 steel crochet hook and insert hook through bead, catch ball strand and draw it back through the bead (see Figure 2). This method is used for wall hangings or door decorations.
(3) If preferred, purchase a wire bead threader at a craft store. After stringing beads on ball strand, be sure to push beads into the ball to keep them out of the way.
(4) To string beads without a wire threader, place end of ball strand on a small cake of beeswax held with fingers of right hand. Use left hand fingers to press down on end of beeswax, pulling end out with the right hand. Repeat until thread end is well waxed and stiff. Be sure to cut waxed end off before starting to tat.

WORKING BEADS INTO PICOTS

Thread JTN with cc. With end of ball strand tat r of 4 ds, slide 2 beads up to JTN, 4 ds, slide 7 beads up to JTN, 4 ds, slide 2 beads up to JTN, 4 ds (see Figure 3). The sts on JTN should look like the illustration; notice the first and third picots have two beads on them, and the middle picot has 7 beads. The middle picot can be threaded with any odd number. End with sson, clr.

If sson seems difficult, it is because of the grouping of stitches with the beads. To ease sson, use left thumb to help push a group of ds off JTN, trying to keep ds as close as possible (see Figure 4). Ch 5 dsb, slide a bead to JTN (when picots are not being joined, one bead can be threaded on JTN using this method). Ch 5 dsb, sson.

R of 4 ds, j to last p **between** two beads of last r, 4 ds. Slide up 3 beads, 4 ds, slide up 2 beads, 4 ds, sson, clr (see Figure 5). Notice the different effect the middle picot gives with three beads. This method makes lovely trims and necklaces.

WORKING BEADS INTO BASE OF RING

A bead can be worked into base of ring either before or after a chain is made. It is easier to work the bead in **after** a ring is completed. Slide a bead up to JTN, anchoring bead and r with right thumb and index finger against JTN in a beginning tatting position to tat a ch. Holding ball strand taut with left hand, wrap ball strand clockwise around JTN once

coming around the bead, lifting thumb and anchoring bead under right thumb. Tat the ch, sson. Proceed with second r and ch, ending with third r (see Figure 6). After sson, notice that working the bead into the base of the r places bead on top of r.

To work a teardrop at base of a r, thread it as follows: Tat all the ds on the JTN for r, sson, but do not clr. Unthread JTN and thread teardrop on cc, sliding to top of cc, rethread JTN and clr.

TO WORK BEADS IN DOUBLE STITCHES BETWEEN PICOTS, NOT IN PICOTS

R of 3 ds, slide 2 beads up, 3 ds, slide 3 beads up, 3 ds, slide 2 beads up, 3 ds, sson, clr. Ch 4 dsb, slide 2 beads up, 4 dsb, sson. R of 3 ds, j between the 2 beads in last p of previous r, 3 ds, slide 1 bead up, 3 ds, slide 1 bead up, 3 ds, slide 3 beads up, 3 ds, slide 1 bead up, 3 ds, slide 1 bead up, 3 ds, slide 2 beads up, 3 ds, sson, clr. Use thumb to help sson, clr. Ch 4 dsb, slide 2 beads, 4 dsb, sson. R of 3 ds, j between 2 beads in last p of previous r, 3 ds, slide 3 beads up, 3 ds, slide 2 beads up, sson, clr (see Figure 7). Note the individual bead between

Fig. 3   Fig. 5   Fig. 7

Fig. 4   Fig. 6   Fig. 8

ds in the upper part of the large r between the beaded picots (see Figure 7).

POSITIONING A BEAD IN THE CENTER OF A RING

Tat a r, sson, clr. Draw ball strand across top of r to middle p, fold strand and thread loop made with ball strand, use the folded 6-inch piece of fine wire to serve as a needle and thread a bead on the loop. If the bead to be used has a larger hole, insert a crochet hook in the hole of bead, catch loop with the hook and draw through bead (see Figure 8). Remove wire.

Fit beaded loop over middle p like a collar. Pull ball strand to tighten the loop on the p to hold the bead on the p, pin with a small safety pin. Later, when working next tatting row, join to the two loops — the beaded loop and the picot and bead will stay in place. When middle p has beads on it, bead is planned for center of the r and another row will not be tatted, string loop from center bead over beaded middle p. Give ball strand a tug to tighten loop under bead or beads in the middle p. They should anchor the center bead in place in the r.

WORKING A BEAD ON A PICOT ANOTHER WAY

Tat a ring making picots to connect to other rings longer than those without beads. Picots threaded in this manner are the first and third picots of a ring, but there are times when the middle picot and those on the chains are threaded too. After the ch and first 4 ds of second r are completed, fold a 6-inch piece of wire, inserting one end through third p of first r. Thread bead on wire and slide it down to p (see Figure 9).

With a size 1 steel crochet hook or size needed for bead and yarn or thread used, insert hook into p where wire is above bead, catch ball strand with hook, drawing it back out of p to form a loop and remove wire. Place loop on JTN and give ball strand a tug to tighten p on JTN. Complete r with 4 ds, p, 4 ds, p, 4 ds, sson, clr. This method of working beads with tatting is a bit slower, but the work looks as nice from the back as from the front.

WORKING BEADS INTO PARALLEL TATTING

There are two ways to work beads into

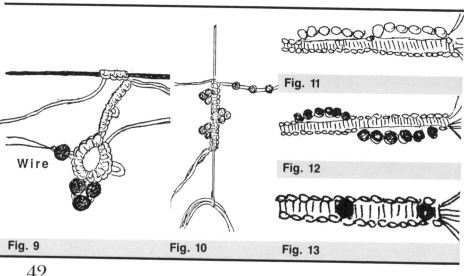

Wire

Fig. 9   Fig. 10   Fig. 11   Fig. 12   Fig. 13

parallel tatting – either on the ball strand or on the carrying cord of parallel cording.

Stringing Beads on Ball Strand

Thread JTN with strand of thread or yarn for cc. Measure 1-1/2 yards of thread or yarn from ball but do not cut. Fold thread or yarn to make a loop. Holding loop of ball strand in left hand, pick up JTN, running it through loop of ball strand and loop of cc, and interlocking the two loops by pulling them "apart." To work beads into parallel tatting, string beads on ball strands. *Ch 1 ds on the left, 1 dsb on the right. Repeat from * twice. Slide 3 beads up to JTN on left, 1 ds. Slide 3 beads up to JTN on right, 1 dsb on right. Slide 3 beads up on left, 1 ds (see Figure 10).

To work beads in left ball strand, string beads on that strand and tat as follows: *Ds on left, dsb on right. Repeat from * twice. **Slide 6 beads up to JTN and note the space taken on JTN. Tat enough dsb st with right strand to take up that space, ending by tatting 1 ds with left strand to secure beads on JTN (see Figure 11). Repeat from ** as desired. Since you already know how many dsb stitches it took to cover the

space along the 6 beads, just tat them and secure the six beads as before.

When beads are worked into ball strands at the same time, any number of beads can be used but must be alternated as follows: Start with (a) to work in the first unit of beads with left strand. (a) After beads are secured with 1 dsb, slide up 6 beads on right. (b) Tat same number of ds on left as on right to fill the space, ending by securing the group of right beads with a ds on JTN (see Figure 12). Repeat (a) and (b) for desired length. Any number of beads desired may be placed on each strand. Group them in three's as in Figure 10 or with three on right strand and five on left strand.

Working Beads into Carrying Cord of Parallel Cording

Thread JTN, attaching ball strand to cc as in ball strand method. Ch 6 ds on left and 6 dsb on right, *sson. Remove JTN, string bead on both ends of cc. Slide bead down to previous ds. Rethread JTN, fold back cc. Place JTN under right thumb and tat alternately 6 more st by repeating from * for length desired (see Figure 13).

PROJECTS

JoAnn's Metallic Gold and Pearl Necklace and Earrings

Begin working beads with tatting in this necklace pattern. Suggestions for other materials to use are given at the end of pattern.

Materials: JTN #00 and threader, embroidery needle and scissors, needle-nose

JIFFY NEEDLE TATTING

Step 3: R of 4 ds, slide 4 beads to JTN for first beaded picot (bp), 8 ds, slide 4 beads to JTN for bp, 4 ds, sson, clr.

Step 4: Ch 6 dsb, slide 4 beads to JTN, 3 dsb, slide 6 beads to JTN, 3 dsb, slide 4 beads to JTN, ending with 6 dsb, sson.

Step 5: R of 4 ds, j to last bp of previous r (insert tip of JTN between 2 middle beads), 8 ds, slide 4 beads to JTN, 4 ds, sson, clr. Repeat Steps 4 and 5 until there are 21 rings and 20 chains in the necklace or for desired length. Remove JTN, sew ends with an embroidery needle, and trim. Attach clasps between middle beads of p at each end of necklace. With needle-nose pliers, pull embroidery needle if it is caught in metallic thread when pulling through ds.

Earrings

Thread JTN with 1 yard of yarn for cc. R of 4 ds, slide 4 beads to JTN, 4 ds, slide 6 beads to JTN, 4 ds, slide 4 beads to JTN, 4 ds, sson, clr. Remove JTN, sew in ends in r with embroidery needle and trim. Attach earring clips to base of r opposite six-beaded p. Repeat for second earring.

Note: This necklace can be made with JTN #0, 2mm pearl beads and DMC #3 pearl cotton in desired color.

pliers, bead needle threader or a 6-inch piece of fine wire to string beads, 21 yards gold metallic yarn, 396 seed pearl beads, necklace clasp and one pair earring clips.

Necklace

Step 1: Thread JTN with 4 yards of metallic yarn for cc, set aside. If the long cc is not manageable, use a 2-yard strand and piece cc as needed.

Step 2: String all 396 seed beads on ball strand with bead threader. Push beads into ball strand a few at a time to make room on strand to work.

Little Christmas Wreath

Materials: JTN #3 and threader, 1/2 yard each dark green and light green 4-ply worsted weight yarn, 4 red corn beads, scissors and embroidery needle.

Step 1: Thread JTN with three Lark's Heads of double strands to make a full daisy. Use double strand dark green for first Lark's Head, and a lighter green for next two double strand Lark's Heads. String 4 red beads on last double strand of JTN. Remember that first and last one-finger dp have no bead and every other time the 1 one-finger dp is made, slide up a bead.

44

USING TWO OR MORE COLORS

There are four ways to use color in Jiffy Needle Tatting: (1) Use a single color throughout entire pattern. (2) Use a single color in each row or round of tatting. (3) Use a different color for rings and chains in each row. (4) Alternate two colors each double stitch on a ring or chain.

The first two methods of color tatting need no further explanation. For the third way of using color, use one color for the rings and another color for the chains. Color used for carrying cord does not matter since double stitches cover it; however, it is preferable to use the same color as the rings.

USING A DIFFERENT COLOR FOR THE RINGS AND CHAINS IN THE SAME ROW

Materials: JTN #3 or #4 and threader, yarn needle and scissors, 1/2 ounce each pink and green 4-ply yarn. **Note:** To keep track of colors used, it is best to work over a table.

Thread JTN with 1-1/2 yards pink yarn for cc, leaving a 2-1/2-inch length. R of 4 ds, 3 p sep by 4 ds, 4 ds, sson, clr. Drop pink ball to the left, away from you. Pick up green, leaving a 2-1/2-inch length. Ch 6 dsb, p, 6 dsb, sson. Drape green over right hand. Pick up pink, drawing pink ball strand across back of r from base of r to middle p. Place JTN

next to ball strand at back of r. Grasp r, ball strand and JTN at r between the middle and third p, r of 4 ds. Release r and ball strand. There is a crossover strand between base of r and 4 ds on JTN (see Figure 1).

Holding r in left hand and JTN in right hand, rotate point of JTN toward you, down under the crossover strand so that crossover strand is now over JTN (see Figure 2). J to last p of previous r, rotate back out and under crossover strand, bringing loop from ball strand with JTN, leaving loop on JTN (see Figure 3).

If joining to third p of previous r under crossover strand seems awkward, use a crochet hook to j to that p by shifting JTN to three fingers of right hand to free right thumb and index finger. Continue holding the previous r in the left hand. Grasp crochet hook with right thumb and index finger, passing hook **under** crossover strand and inserting hook in last p of previous r to j to p. Draw ball strand loop out of p, from under crossover strand, bringing it up and around, slip it onto JTN. Remove hook, give ball strand a tug with left hand to tighten loop on JTN (see Figure 3).

R of 4 ds, 2 p sep by 4 ds, 4 ds, sson, clr (see Figure 4). For next ch, drop pink, pick up green over right hand. Pull strand left, 6 dsb, p, 6 dsb, sson, replace strand over right hand. Remember green strand must always be above and to the

Fig. 1   Fig. 2   Fig. 3

right of JTN to keep it separate from pink strand.

Putting two colors in same row of tatting works when the rings follow each other in a series. If there is a break in the series of rings, it is necessary to cut pink ball strand, leaving a 2-1/2-inch length. At next ring, leave a 2-1/2-inch length and start again with pink, working in ends later.

To put a different color in the rings from the chain, make each ring, cut pink strand and work in ends; it is not necessary to cut ch strand. To make next ring, begin again to make the ring and cut yarn, working in two ends in each ring.

PROJECTS

Two-Color Marigold Coaster
One Color Each Row

Fig. 4

Materials: JTN #3 and threader, yarn needle and scissors, 1/4 ounce each pink and white 4-ply yarn.

Step 1 − Center Daisy: Thread JTN with 20 inches of pink for cc. Measure

1-1/2 yards pink, do not cut, but fold at that point. Attach loop to JTN with Lark's Head. R of 12 two-finger dp, sson, clr. Remove JTN, work in ends and trim.

Step 2: Thread JTN with 2-1/2 yards white for cc. R of 3 ds, 1 one-finger p, 3 ds, j to any dp in daisy (right side facing), 3 ds, 1 one-finger p, 3 ds, sson, clr. Ch 9 dsb, sson. *R of 3 ds, j to last p in previous r, 3 ds, j to next dp in daisy, 3 ds, 1 one-finger p, 3 ds, sson, clr. Ch 9 dsb, sson. Repeat from * 9 times, r of 3 ds, j to last p in previous r, 3 ds, j to next dp (last one) in daisy, 3 ds, j to first p of first r at beginning of rnd, 3 ds, sson, clr. Ch 9 dsb, sson. Run JTN up center of r, between strands of cc, and secure ch to base of r. Remove JTN, sew in ends and trim.

Step 3: Thread JTN with 2-1/2 yards pink for cc. Attach cc to base of any r of previous rnd. Run JTN up center of r, through loop of cc, and secure cc to r. With pink *4 dsb, 1 one-finger p, 2 dsb, 1 one-finger p, 2 dsb, 1 one-finger p, 4 dsb, sson. Run JTN up center of r to left (right side facing), between strands of cc, and secure ch to p. Repeat from * 11 times. Remove JTN, work in ends and trim.

Four-Leaf Clover Coaster

This coaster shows two methods of working two colors in the same row or round. The rings of first round are not in a series, so it is necessary to cut the color after each ring is completed and start again for next ring. The pink rings of second round are in a series, and can be tatted using the crossover strand from ring to ring method. The green chains are continuous in each round.

Materials: JTN #4 and threader, yarn needle and scissors, 1/2 ounce each green and pink 4-ply yarn.

Step 1 – Center Ring: Thread JTN with 2 yards of green for cc. Using green and leaving a 2-inch length, r of 2 ds, 11 p sep by 2 ds, sson, clr. Do not cut yarn, but work in end length.

Rnd 1: With green, 6 dsb, p, 3 dsb, p, 3 dsb, p, 3 dsb, sson. Drape green strand over right hand and place green ball out of the way. With pink, *leave a 2-inch length, r of 3 ds, p, 3 ds, j to first p to right of counterclockwise ch around center r. Be sure knot side of center r is facing. Ds, j to next p in center r, 3 ds, p, 3 ds, sson, clr. Cut pink 2 inches from r, work in ends and trim.

Pull green strand from right hand to the left and across to position green for next ch. Ch 3 dsb, p, 3 dsb, p, 3 dsb, p, 6 dsb, sson. Run JTN up next p, between strands of cc, and secure on p (rnp). Avoid pull on picot. Turn work clockwise, bring cc toward you, under green and across work. Ch 6 dsb, j to last p of previous ch, 3 dsb, p, 3 dsb, p, 3 dsb, sson. Place green back over right hand. Repeat from * three times.

In last ch when turning the work clockwise, after ch 6 dsb, bring first ch at beginning of rnd around coaster clockwise to JTN. Fold ch toward you

down against center r. J to third p in that ch, 6 dsb, sson. Straighten clover, run JTN through center of center r, between strands of cc, and secure ch to center r next to first ch (rnr). Remove JTN, work in ends and trim.

Rnd 2: (This round is a series of 16 rings with no break in the round.) Draw pink across back of previous r to line up with middle p. With JTN, the pink r, and ball strand between right thumb and index finger at r between middle and third p, r of 3 ds. Release previous r and notice crossover strand between base of r and 4 ds on JTN. Rotate point of JTN toward you, under crossover strand, j to last p of previous r. Rotate JTN under and out from crossover strand bridging ball strand with JTN to form loop on JTN. Use right index finger to hold ball strand loop on JTN as JTN is rotated from crossover strand.

R of 3 ds, p, 3 ds, p, 3 ds, sson, clr. Drop pink to the left from JTN. Pick up green from right hand, draw it to the left and repeat from * 15 times. In last r, j last p to first p in first r. Cut pink 2 inches from last r, ending with ch 10 dsb, sson. Run JTN up center of first r at beginning of rnd, between strands of cc — (rnr). Remove JTN and work in ends.

MAKING DOUBLE PICOT DAISIES USING TWO OR THREE COLORS

DAISIES WITH TWO COLORS

When using two colors for daisies, two double ball strands and either one-finger or three-finger picots are used in making double picots (dp).

Step 1: Thread JTN with 24 inches pink for cc.

Step 2: Measure 2-1/2 yards pink from ball — do not cut, but fold at that point and attach to JTN with a Lark's Head. Measure 2 yards of white, do not cut, but fold it and attach to JTN with a Lark's

Head. Measure back and cut opposite end evenly to match first strand (see Figure 5).

Step 3: *Pull two pink strands with left hand from the back of JTN, over three fingers, making 1 one-finger dp. Drop strands, remove fingers and slide ds up to Lark's Head. From front of JTN and white strands, make a one-finger dp. Drop the white and remove finger. Repeat from * until there are 8 dp of each color, sson.

It's best to begin with the longer dp and end with the shorter dp so the daisy will have an even number of dp in each color (see Figure 6). Close daisy, sson, clr (see Figure 7). Turn daisy over, sew 3 ends in r one direction, other 3 ends opposite and trim.

FULLER PICOT DAISIES USING THREE COLORS

Three-Color Double Picot Wreath
 Materials: JTN #3 and threader, 4-ply yarns in the following amounts and colors: 1 yard red, 8 yards dark green, 7 yards medium green, 5 yards light green, scissors.
 Step 1: Thread JTN with 30 inches of 4-ply red yarn for cc.
 Step 2: Measure 8 yards dark green 4-ply yarn, do not cut but fold in half and attach to JTN with a Lark's Head. Cut ends to equal length. Measure 3-1/2 yards of medium green yarn, do not cut, but double it, attach to JTN with a Lark's Head and slide it up next to the dark green Lark's Head, cut ends. Measure 5 yards of light green yarn, do not cut, but double it and attach it to JTN with Lark's Head and slide next to other two Lark's Head Knots. Cut all strands evenly.
 *Holding JTN in right hand, with left hand bring dark green double strand forward toward front of JTN and make one 4-finger dp. Drop dark green double strand, remove 4 fingers and slide ds up to last Lark's Head. With the medium green double strand between dark and light green strands, draw medium green forward across front of dark green dp, making one 3-finger p on JTN. Drop medium green, remove fingers and slide ds up to dark green ds. Bring light green double strand across front of all previous work, making 1 one-finger dp on JTN. Drop light green double strand, remove index finger and slide ds next to previous medium green ds. Repeat from * 9 times, sson, clr. Remove JTN.
 Thread yarn needle with one end of red and stitch into circle of knots to secure r. Make a small bow with red ends. Trim green ends even with longest dp. Do not cut loops.
 Note: To string beads on wreath, string them on shortest strands together (in this instruction the light green strands). Trim ends of bow a bit longer than the longest double (dark green) picots. These make wonderful package trims. Try making them with other colors such as 3 shades of pink. To crochet daisies together be sure the daisies have a multiple of 4 double picots.

Fig. 5

Fig. 6   **Fig. 7**

COMBINING JIFFY NEEDLE TATTING WITH OTHER NEEDLEWORK

This chapter explains combining Jiffy Needle Tatting with crochet, hand and/or machine knitting, serging and embroidery. The chapter is divided into four sections: 1. Crochet; 2. Knitting by hand or machine; 3. Serging; 4. Embroidery and Appliqué.

TATTING WITH CROCHET

It is relatively obvious how tatted edgings can be combined with crochet, but some explanation will help to understand how insertions are incorporated. The easiest and most accurate way to proceed is to first make a tatted sample of the insertion motif to be used. Then make a swatch of the crochet pattern a bit longer than the tatted sample. Place tatted sample over crochet swatch, count number of crochet rows to equal the width of tatted insertion and note number of rows. If total insertion is to be joined by the rings, count number of crochet stitches visible between the rings from the middle picot of one ring to the middle picot of next ring. If the motif is joined by chains, count the visible crochet stitches between the picots of one chain to picots of next chain and note the number. When planning a garment, counting in this manner ensures a better fit. Counting stitches and rows is not as critical for afghans, scarves and shawls but it does help.

PROJECT

Hydie's Treasure Bag

Counting rows in this pattern is not as important as counting stitches. This bag measures 9 inches in diameter.

Gauge: 4 double stitches equal one inch

Materials: JTN #5 and threader, yarn needle and scissors, 3 skeins navy blue and 2 skeins white rug yarn, 1-1/2 yards white cord, 10 white 3/4-inch carbone rings, size G crochet hook, 1/3 yard blue fabric for lining, 10 straight pins, needle and matching thread.

Base of Bag: With crochet hook and navy yarn, ch 4, sc in first ch to form ring.

Rnd 1: Ch 3, 12 dc in ring, sl st in top st of first ch at beginning of rnd.

Rnd 2: Ch 3, 2 ds in each dc of previous rnd, catching both sides of st, sl st in top ch at beginning of rnd.

Rnd 3: Ch 3, dc in same st, *2 dc in next st, dc in next st. Repeat from * around to ch, sl st in top st.

Rnd 4: Ch 3, dc in next 3 st beginning with same st as ch. *2 Dc in next st, dc in next 3 sts. Repeat from * around to ch, sl st in top ch.

Rnd 5: Repeat Rnd 4.

Rnd 6: Ch 3, dc in same st, dc in next 3 sts. *2 Dc in next st, dc in next 4 sts. Repeat from * around to ch, sl st in top of ch. Do not cut yarn.

Sides of Bag: Rnd 1: Ch 2, sc in each st around to ch (catching only back loop of st), sl st in top of ch.

Rnd 2: Ch 2, sc in each sc of previous rnd (catching both loops of st), sl st in top st of ch. Fasten off, work in ends and trim.

First Tatted Rnd: Thread JTN with 2-1/2 yards of white yarn for cc. R of 3 ds, p, 3 ds, j to any sc of previous rnd, catching both loops of sc st, 3 ds, p, 3 ds, sson, clr. Ch 4 dsb, p, 4 dsb, sson. *R of 3 ds, j to last p of previous r, 3 ds, sk 2 sc of previous rnd, 3 ds, p, 3 ds, sson. Ch 4 dsb, p, 4 dsb, sson. Repeat from * around to within last 5 dc sts of previous rnd. Ch 3 ds, j to last p of first r at beginning of rnd, 2 ds, sson, clr. Ch 4 dsb, p, 4 dsb, sson. Run JTN up center of first r, between strands of cc, and secure ch to base of r − (rnr). Remove JTN, work in ends and trim.

Middle Crochet Strip: Rnd 1: With crochet hook and navy yarn j to p of any ch of previous rnd as follows: *With both thumbs, open p and j to tatted ch in groove of p with sc, ch 2, repeat from * in p of each ch around. Sl st in first sc of first tatted ch. Do not cut yarn.

Rnd 2: Ch 2, sc st in each ch and sc around, and sl st in first top ch at beginning of rnd.

Rnd 3: Ch 3, dc in each sc of previous rnd − catching both sides of st, sl st in top of ch.

Rnd 4: Repeat Rnd 2. Fasten off, work in ends and trim.

Second Tatted Rnd: Repeat first tatted rnd.

Rnd 5: Repeat middle crochet strip three times. Do not cut yarn.

Attaching Carbone Rings: Rnd 1: Ch 2, sc in same st as ch. Count sts around

top of bag and divide sts to space 10 carbone rings evenly around bag. Attach a straight pin to mark points to attach the rings. *Pull ball strand up through first carbone ring to form loop and place loop on hook. Turn ring to the right and anchor under right thumb against edge of bag, pull ball strand to tighten ring to bag, sc in next st on edge of bag. Sc in next few sts to next marked point, remove pin. Repeat from * until all carbone rings are attached. Sc in each of last sts. Sl st in top st of ch at beginning of rnd.

Rnd 2: Ch 2, sc in each st around, ending with sl st in top st of ch at beginning of rnd. Fasten off, work in ends and trim.

Tatted Rim Of Bag: Thread JTN with 2-1/2 yards navy yarn for cc. R of 3 ds, p, 3 ds, j to any sc of previous rnd, catching both sides of st, 3 ds, p, 3 ds, sson, clr. Ch 8 dsb, sson. *R of 3 ds, j to last p of previous r, 3 ds, sk 2 dc on edge of bag, j to next st, 3 ds, p, 3 ds, sson, clr. Ch 8 dsb, sson. Repeat from * around to within last 5 sc on edge of bag. R of 3 ds, j to left p in previous r, 3 ds, sk 2 st in previous r, 3 ds, j to first p in first r at beginning of rnd, 3 ds, sson, clr. Ch 8 dsb, sson. J ch to base of r (rnr). Remove JTN, work in ends and trim.

Lining: Cut a circle of paper the same diameter as bottom of bag. When pinning paper to fabric, cut 1/2 inch from edge of circle around paper pattern and set aside. From the inside, measure side of bag from bottom to the carbone rings and measure around the circle adding 2 inches (see Figure 1). Measurement is the length and width for the side lining. To sew lining, fold long rectangle so that one end is 1/2 inch longer than the other. Baste together and sew by hand or machine.

Open fabric and insert a book or a magazine under seam to stabilize work. Fold long end over short end and fold the two together again to conceal raw edge, pin and hem by hand or machine, making a French seam. Pin sides to bottom of bag (circle) wrong side out. Add bias tape or stretch lace around edge of bottom, easing when repinning. Baste and sew by hand or machine. Pin bias tape up the side and around bag to conceal raw bottom edges, sew by hand. Turn bag to wrong side to fit lining over bag. Tack lining around bottom of bag, folding in top lining edge in line with carbone rings, and hem around bag. Turn bag to right side.

Cut cord in half, lace through rings one way and sew two ends together with navy yarn to prevent fraying. Run other cord the opposite direction through carbone rings and sew ends together. This bag can also be made with Jiffy Tatting Needles Sizes 0, 1, 2, 3 or 4 and suggested threads or yarns. Remember that a smaller JTN and finer thread result in a smaller bag. Follow instructions on thread or yarn labels for laundering and hang upside down to dry.

COMBINING DAISY MEDALLIONS WITH CROCHET

Daisy medallions are fun to make and can be made into any size by using a different number of fingers. The projects in this section utilize daisy motifs in Wagon Wheel, Granny Square and the Butterfly Motif.

Wagon Wheel Daisy

Materials: JTN #3 and threader, size G crochet hook, 2 yards 4-ply yarn, yarn needle and scissors.

Step 1: Make a daisy motif of 12 three-finger double picots (dp) (see Chapter II if needed).

Step 2: Using a size G crochet hook, edge daisy with a simple ch for a border. *Single crochet (sc) into any dp. Be sure the knotted side of daisy is facing (see Figure 2). Ch 3 and repeat from * 15 times, ending ch 3 and slip stitch (sl st) into the first sc st. This completes the Wagon Wheel Daisy. If the daisy cups, the chain is too tight, so use a larger crochet hook.

To join a second wagon wheel, sc in any dp of second daisy. Ch 1 (be sure daisies are back to back), sl st in middle ch of any ch of first daisy. Ch 1, sc in next dp of second daisy. Continue edging second daisy, ending sl st in first sc. Edge and join third daisy in the same manner.

Granny Square Daisy

Materials: JTN #3 and threader, size G crochet hook, 2 yards 4-ply yarn, yarn needle and scissors.

Long Side
Stitching
Short Side
Fold

| Fig. 1 | Fig. 2 | Fig. 3 |

Make a daisy motif of 12 three-finger dp. With size G crochet hook, sc in any 2 dp (4 loops), ch 2, *2 dc in the next 2 dp, ch 3, 2 dc in the same 2 dp – first corner complete. Ch 2, sc in next 2 dp, ch 2 – side complete. Repeat from * three times, always in next p, ending sl st in first sc at beginning of edging. Fasten off, sew in ends and trim (see Figure 3). Sew these Granny Squares together for scarves, afghans and stoles.

Daisy Butterfly Motif

Materials: JTN #4 and threader, yarn needle, size J crochet hook, scissors and 4-ply yarn in the following colors and amounts: 18 inches pink, two 18-inch strands blue, 4 yards pink, two 4-yard strands blue, one ounce white for crocheted edging.

Step 1: Thread JTN with 18-inch pink strand for cc. Double 4-yard strand of pink and attach it to JTN with a Lark's Head. Make *6 three-fingered dp. Make 1 fingertip dp and repeat from * once, sson, clr. Work ends into knots on wrong side of daisy (knot side is right side), set aside. Make two more butterflies using blue strands.

Step 2 – Assembling Butterflies: Row 1: With hook and white yarn hold a blue butterfly, knot side facing, and connect first three-fingered dp (at left of one of the fingertip dp) with 1 sc in that three-finger dp. *Ch 1, sc in next three-fingered dp. Repeat from * 4 times. **Ch 5, sl st in next fingertip p, ch 3. With knot side facing, pick up pink butterfly, sl st in a fingertip dp, ch 3, sc back to 2nd st of 5th ch st of previous butterfly, ch 1, sc in first three-finger dp of second butterfly. *Ch 1, sc in the next three-finger dp, repeat from * four times. Repeat from ** adding second blue butterfly and more if desired. Turn string of butterflies and crochet opposite side in same manner.

Row 2: With hook and white yarn, *sc in ch between first and second dp of first blue butterfly, ch 3, dc in every ch of first row across wings of butterflies sep by 1 ch st between sts. Turn strip and repeat second row on opposite side. Sew strips together with tapestry needle by matching wings and stitches with an overhand st, catching inside edge of stitch to inside edge of st on opposite side.

COMBINING JIFFY NEEDLE TATTING WITH KNITTING

Since there are different things to consider when combining tatting with hand knitting vs. machine knitting, instructions for each are given separately.

Hand Knit Articles

Add your own personal touch to this sweater set with tatted insertions for the cardigan and a matching tatted yoke for the shell.

PROJECT

Knit Sweater Set with Jiffy Needle Tatting Inserts

Knit instructions for the shell and cardigan are given for small size with medium and large sizes in parentheses. The set is knit of 3-ply sport weight yarn, 7 ounces for the shell and 14 ounces for the cardigan. Use circular knitting needles numbers 4 and 6 and a set of number 4 double-pointed needles. In addition, you'll need stitch markers, small safety pins, 8-inch stitch holders, a size F crochet hook and seven 5/8-inch pearl buttons. For the tatted yoke, a JTN #2, a yarn needle and scissors.

Gauge: 6 sts equal 1 inch
8 rows equal 1 inch
TO SAVE TIME, TAKE TIME TO CHECK GAUGE.
CARDIGAN
This raglan cardigan is worked from the neck down; tatted insertions are on the front edges and above the sleeve ribbings.

With larger 29-inch circular needle, cast on 80 sts.

Row 1: P 14 (left front), place marker, p 1 (left front seam st), p 10 (left sleeve), place marker, p 1 (left back seam st), p 28 (back), place marker, p 1 (right back seam st), p 10 (right sleeve), place marker, p 1 (right front seam st), p 14 (right front).

Row 2: K 13, inc in next st, sl marker, k 1, sl marker, inc in next st, k 8, inc in next st, sl marker. K 1, sl marker, inc in next st, k 26, inc in next st, sl marker, k 1, sl marker, inc in next st, k 8, inc in next st, sl marker, k 1, sl marker, inc in next st, k 13 − 8 inc.

Row 3: P each st. Repeat Rows 2 and 3, inc one st in st before and after markers at each seam until there are: Each front 42 (44,46) sts, each sleeve 66 (70,88) sts, back 84 (88,92) sts, seam sts 4 (4,4). Total number of sts 304 (320,336).

BODY: K front panel sts, remove marker, k seam st, remove marker, sl left sleeve sts to a holder, remove marker. Cast on 4 sts for left underarm, k seam st, remove marker, k all back sts, remove marker. K seam st, remove marker, sl right sleeve sts to a holder, cast on 4 sts for right underarm, k right front sts − 180 (188,196) sts.

*P one row, k one row. Repeat from * until sweater measures 14 inches or desired length from underarm.

Change to smaller needles for ribbing.
Row 1: K 1, p 1 across row.
Row 2: P 1, k 1 across row.
Repeat Rows 1 and 2 for 2 inches. Bind off, work in ends.

SLEEVES: Sl sts of one sleeve to larger 16-inch circular needle (or evenly divide the sts on 3 double-pointed needles).

Rnd 1: K sleeve sts around to underarm, k 2 underarm sts, place marker on needle, k 2 underarm sts.

Continue knitting around, slipping marker each rnd until sleeve length is 2-3/4 inches above wrist. Remove marker and bind off sts. Repeat for other sleeve.

Foundation for Front Insertion: A crocheted foundation is worked here to keep edge straight and firm. At left front panel, with crochet hook and yarn, begin at top corner st and sc down front to last st of ribbing. Fasten off. With right side of front facing, begin at first st of ribbing and sc to top k st. Be sure there are the same number of sc in each front.

Tatted Insertion: Thread JTN with 3 yards yarn for cc (piece cc as needed). Remember all picots are tiny picots (tp), about 1/4 inch on JTN.

R of 3 ds, p, 3 ds, with left front facing, j to 3rd sc from top (catch both loops of st each time you j), 3 ds, p, 3 ds, sson, clr.

*Ch 4 dsb, p, 4 dsb, sson. R of 3 ds, j to last p of previous r, 3 ds, sk 2 sts on panel edge, j to next st, 3 ds, p, 3 ds, sson, clr. Repeat from * down front edge to last 2 ribbing sts. Remove JTN, work in ends and trim.

Turn sweater, right side facing and repeat, working from bottom ribbing up to top edge.

Ribbing for Left Front: Row 1: With right side facing, insert hook and sc in 2nd sc from top st of foundation. Ch 1, sc in first p of first r, ch 5. *With thumbs, open p in first tatted ch, j to p with sc, ch 2. Repeat from * down panel edge, ending with ch 5 for corner, sc in last p of last r, ch 1, sl st in next to last st of foundation, fasten off.

Row 2: At top of left front with smaller needles, begin at 4th st and pick up one st in every ch and sc along edge, ending

in 2nd ch of bottom corner. Turn sweater and work in k 1, p 1 ribbing across row. Repeat row until ribbing is 3/4 inch. Bind off on right side leaving an 18-inch length at bottom ribbing before cutting yarn.

With crochet hook, sc across bottom

of ribbing. Sc in 3 ch sts, sc in sc in p of last r, sc in next ch, sl st in last foundation st at end of panel. Fasten off.

Ribbing for Right Front: With smaller needles, repeat ribbing for right front. Leaving 18-inch length yarn, begin in 4th ch at bottom, pick up sts along edge to 4th ch in top corner. Work 5 rows, working 7 buttonholes spaced at equal intervals by k 1, p 1, *bind off 2 sts, continue ribbing to next buttonhole. Repeat from * 6 times.

Next Row: Work ribbing to buttonhole bind off, *cast on 2 sts and continue ribbing and repeat from * across row. Work 2 more rows ribbing. Bind off.

Neck Ribbing: With smaller needles working from right to left, pick up 4 sts at end of front ribbing (starting in 2nd st), one st in each ch st and sc around p of top r, 14 right front sts, 10 sleeve sts, 28 back sts, 10 sleeve sts, 14 left front sts. Pick up one st in ch sts on each side of p of first r, 4 sts across end of left front ribbing. Work in ribbing (k 1, p 1) for 4 rows, bind off on right side, leaving a 12-inch yarn length. Pick up yarn length with hook and work into ribbing. Repeat with yarn length at other side.

Tatted Insertion and Sleeve Ribbing: Weave in yarn length from sleeve. Bind off. Thread JTN with 3 yards yarn.

R of 3 ds, p, 3 ds, j to right side of sleeve at left of yarn end, 3 ds, p, 3 ds, sson, clr. Ch 4 dsb, p, 4 dsb, sson.

*R of 3 ds, j to last p of previous r, 3 ds, sk 2 sts on sleeve edge, j to next st, 3 ds, p, 3 ds, sson, clr. Ch 4 dsb, p, 4 dsb, sson. Repeat from * around sleeve to last 5 sts. R of 3 ds, j to last p of previous r, 3 ds, sk 2 sts on sleeve edge, j to next st, 3 ds, j to first p in first r, 3 ds, sson, clr.

Sleeve Ribbing: With yarn and hook, *j in p that falls at inside of wrist with sc and ch 1. Repeat from * around tatted ch, working from right to left, ending ch 1, sl st in sc at beginning of rnd. Do not fasten off.

Using 3 double-pointed needles, pick up one st in each sc and ch around sleeve, dividing them evenly on the needles. Work in ribbing (k 1, p 1) for 2 inches. Bind off and work in ends.

To finish, sew buttons opposite buttonholes, block sweater following label directions.

SHELL

With smaller needles, cast on 172 (180,188) sts, place a stitch marker to mark rnd. Making sure sts do not twist, work around in ribbing (k 1, p 1) until ribbing measures 2-1/2 inches.

BODY: Change to larger needles, sl first marker, k 4, place marker, k 82 (86,90), place marker, k 4, place marker, k to first marker. K around evenly for one inch above ribbing. *Inc in first st **after first and third markers** and in the last st **before second and fourth markers.** K around evenly for 1 inch. Repeat from * 6 times — 16 sts between markers for sides of shell. K around un-

til shell measures 12-1/2 inches or desired length from beginning of ribbing.

Divide Sts for Front and Back: Remove first marker, k 3, bind off 10 sts, k 3, remove 2nd marker, k to 3rd marker, remove it, k 3, bind off 10 sts, k 3, remove 4th marker and k remaining sts.

First Panel of Shell: Row 1: Turn work, p across.

Row 2: K 2 tog, k across to last 2 sts, k 2 tog. Repeat Rows 1 and 2 until work measures 3 inches from armhole, bind off. Bind off all sts, leaving a 2-yard length. Repeat Rows 1 and 2 for second panel.

Crocheted Foundation for Armhole: On right side, with crochet hook and length of yarn at armhole, sc around armhole from top point of one panel to top of other panel. Fasten off. Repeat for other armhole, making sure each armhole foundation has same number sc.

Tatted Yoke: Note: Work yoke the same for front and back.

Thread JTN with 3 yards yarn for cc. (Piece cc as needed.)

Rnd 1: Note: Tiny picots (tp) are used throughout yoke. R of 3 ds, 3 p sep by 3 ds, 3 ds, sson, clr. Place pin in this r. Ch 4 dsb, sson. With shell right side out working from left to right at one panel, j to 3rd st from left corner of panel along top edge (Figure 4, Arrow 1) by running

JTN from back to front under sides of st, between strands of cc, and securing ch to st. *Ch 4 dsb, sson. R of 3 ds, j to last p of previous r, 3 ds, p, 3 ds, p, 3 ds, sson, clr. Ch 4 dsb, sson. Sk 3 sts at edge of panel, j to next st. Repeat from * across panel to 3rd st from corner. Ch 4 dsb, sson. R of 3 ds, j to last p of previous r, 3 ds, p, 3 ds, p, 3 ds, sson, clr. Place second pin in this r. Do not cut cc.

Working over Shoulder (Straps): Ch 4 dsb, p, 4 dsb, sson. *R of 3 ds, j to last p of previous r, 3 ds, p, 3 ds, p, 3 ds, sson, clr. Ch 4 dsb, p, 4 dsb, sson. Repeat from * 11 (12,13) times.

Repeat Rnd 1 so both front and back panels are the same. Repeat shoulder strap for second shoulder.

Rnd 2: Thread JTN with 3 yards yarn for cc (piece as needed).

R of 3 ds, 3 p sep by 3 ds, 3 ds, sson, clr (Figure 4, Arrow 2). Ch 3 dsb, sson. With shell right side out at left r marked by pin, count to left from marked r to second r, j to middle p, rnp, 3 dsb, sson, j to next r at left of that r, 3 dsb, sson. R of 3 ds, j to last p of previous r, 3 ds, p, 3 ds, sson, clr. Ch 3 dsb, sson, j to p in marked r, rnp. Move pin to middle p of previous r in second rnd. Ch 3 dsb, sson, j to p in next r of previous rnd, 3 dsb, sson. R of 3 ds, j to last p of previous r, 3 ds, p, 3 ds, p, 3 ds, sson, clr. Ch 4 dsb, sson, j to p in next r of previous rnd, rnp. Ch 4 dsb, sson.

*R of 3 ds, j to last p of previous r, 3 ds, p, 3 ds, p, 3 ds, sson, clr. Ch 4 dsb, sson, j to p in next r of previous rnd, rnp, 4 dsb, sson. R of 3 ds, j to last p of previous r, 3 ds, p, 3 ds, p, 3 ds, sson, clr. Repeat from * across panel to r at left

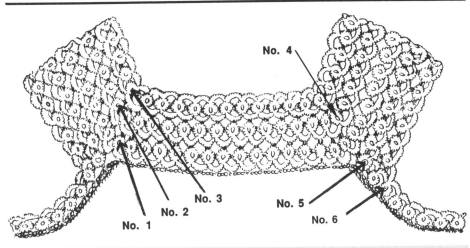

No. 4

No. 3

No. 2

No. 1

No. 5

No. 6

Fig. 4

of second marked r of previous rnd. Ch 3 dsb, sson, j to r at left, rnp. Ch 3 dsb, sson. J to marked r, rnp, 3 dsb, sson. R of 3 ds, j to last p of previous r, 3 ds, p, 3 ds, p, 3 ds, sson, clr. Move pin marker to this r. Ch 3 dsb, sson, j to p in next r of previous rnd, rnp. Ch 3 dsb, sson, j to p in next r of previous rnd, rnp, 3 dsb, sson. R of 3 ds, j to last p of previous r, 3 ds, p, 3 ds, p, 3 ds, sson, clr. (Note: Two rings each are connected to two previous chains).

Ch 4 dsb, sson, j to p in next r of previous rnd, rnp. Ch 4 dsb, sson. *R of 3 ds, j to last p of previous r, 3 ds, p, 3 ds, p, 3 ds, sson, clr. Ch 4 dsb, sson, j to p in next r of previous rnd, rnp, 4 dsb, sson. Repeat from * over the shoulder to within 2 r of the marked r on other panel. Repeat last 2 paragraphs and j last ch to base of first r at beginning of rnd. Remove JTN, work in ends and trim.

Rnd 3: Thread JTN with 3 yards yarn for cc. R of 3 ds, 3 p sep by 3 ds, 3 ds, sson, clr (Figure 4, Arrow 3). Ch 3 dsb. At yoke with r marked with pin, move pin to middle r between 2 ch. J to middle p in r at right of marked r. Ch 3 dsb, j to middle p of next r to left of marked r. Ch 3 dsb, sson. (Note: Three rings are connected to one chain. This gives shape to the neckline). Turn work counterclockwise, bringing cc to back of work.

*R of 3 ds, j to last p ot previous r of 3rd rnd, 3 ds, p, 3 ds, p, 3 ds, sson, clr. Turn work clockwise, bringing cc toward you, under ball strand and across previous r. Ch 4 dsb, j to middle p in next r of previous rnd, 4 dsb, sson. Turn work counterclockwise, bringing cc to back of work. Repeat from * across yoke to next point where the next set of 3 r above 2 ch will be connected (Figure 4, Arrow 4). Repeat the 2 paragraphs of Rnd 3 around yoke. J last ch to base of first r at beginning of rnd, rnr. Remove JTN, work in ends and trim.

Rnd 4: This round is a chain to finish yoke. Thread JTN with 3 yards yarn for cc. J to middle p of any r (right side out) by opening p with thumbs. Run JTN through r, through loop of cc and secure cc to open p.

*Ch 8 dsb, sson. J to next r at left by opening middle p, running JTN through center of p toward you, between strands of cc, and securing to p. Repeat from * around neckline and back to first p at beginning of rnd. Remove JTN, work in ends and trim.

Armhole Border: Rnd 1: R of 3 ds, 3 ds, with yoke right side out, j to top sc in right corner of panel, 3 ds, j to p in ch of first rnd, 3 ds, p, ds, sson, clr (Figure 4, Arrow 5). Ch 4 dsb, p, 4 dsb, sson.

*R of 3 ds, j to last p of previous r, 3 ds, j to p in next ch, 3 ds, p, 3 ds, sson, clr. Ch 4 dsb, p, 4 dsb, sson. Repeat from * to last p of ch connected to the sc in the corner; R of 3 ds, j to last p of previous r, 3 ds, j to p in last ch of previous rnd, 3 ds, j to sc in corner of panel, 3 ds, p, 3 ds, sson, clr. Ch 4 dsb, p, 4 dsb, sson.

*R of 3 ds, j to last p of previous r, 3 ds, sk 3 sts on edge of armhole, 3 ds, p, 3 ds, sson, clr. Ch 8 dsb, sson. Repeat from * along armhole to last 6 sts from other panel corner. R of 3 ds, j to last p of previous r, 3 ds, sk 3 sts, j to next st on edge of panel. Ch 3 ds, j to first p in first r with 4 p, 3 ds, sson, clr. Ch 4 dsb, p, 4 dsb, sson. J ch to base of first r with 4 p at beginning of rnd, rnr. Remove JTN, work in ends and trim.

Rnd 2: Thread JTN with 3 yards of yarn for cc. With yoke facing, begin at right side by running JTN through center of r at right of r with 4 p. Run JTN through loop of cc and secure cc to base of r (Figure 4, Arrow 6).

Ch 8 dsb, sson. R of 3 ds, j to p in first ch at left of r with 4 p, 3 ds, j to p in next ch, 3 ds, j to p in next ch, 3 ds, p, 3 ds, sson, clr. Ch 8 dsb, sson.

*R of 3 ds, j to last p of previous r, 3 ds, j to p in next ch of previous rnd, 3 ds, p, 3 ds, sson, clr. Ch 8 dsb, sson. Repeat from * to last 3 ch with p. R of

3 ds, j to last p of previous r, 3 ds, j to p in next ch, 3 ds, j to p in next ch, 3 ds, j to p in next ch, 3 ds, sson, clr. Ch 8 dsb, sson. J to base of next r, rnr. Remove JTN, work in ends and trim. Repeat for other armhole.

Block shell following label directions.

Machine Knit Articles

A simple tatted chain or an ornate insertion made with the Jiffy Tatting Needle seems to be the perfect answer in assembling knit panels. Keep in mind that most knitting machines have tension bars that keep stitches even and sides straight; however, some do not have a tension bar. When pieces from a knitting machine without a tension bar are used, it is best to crochet one row of single crochet stitches along each side of the panel before the tatting is done.

Tatting Panels Together Made on a Knitting Machine with or without a Tension Bar:

Step 1: Knit the panels in the pattern and color desired for article, work in ends and trim. Each panel must have the same number of stitches and rows.

Step 2: Thread JTN with 3 yards of yarn for cc. Place panel right side up across your lap. Attach cc at top right end of side away from you by running JTN between two top st (see Figure 5, Number 1) back through loop of cc, securing cc to edge of panel. *Ch 3 dsb, p, (if yarn is strong enough a single p is sufficient, but if yarn breaks easily, use twin picots). Ch 3 dsb, sson. Line tatted ch along the side of the panel to determine how far the ch should be attached to the edge. For example, if it takes 8 rows (see Figure 5, Number 2) count back 3 or 4 rows to allow for stitches in the article (see Figure 5, Number 3). Run JTN between the two sts, between two strands of cc, and secure ch to edge of panel. Repeat from * along edge to other end of panel. Piece cc as needed, work in ends and trim.

Step 3: Place first panel on your lap, wrong side up and the side with the tat-

ted chains away from you. Thread JTN with 3 yards of yarn for cc. Place second panel over first panel, right side up (the two panels are back to back). Attach cc to right end of second panel as for first panel in Step 1. *Ch 3 dsb, j to p of first ch in first panel – if there are twin p, j them together or individually. If only one p in the ch you may add strength to p by using your thumbs to open p and j to the open p – ch 3 dsb, sson.

Attach ch to second panel as in first panel. Repeat from * to end of panel, piecing cc as needed. Remove JTN, work in ends and trim. Repeat Step 2 to join remaining panels. Complete panels by tatting an edging of rings and chains along the longer edge.

If you wish, attach fringe to the ends.

Fig. 5

Fig. 6

PROJECT

Diamond Lap Robe

This lap robe is made on a knitting machine with no tension bars.

Step 1: Knit panels of 4-ply yarn on knitting machine. Each panel has a row of lace diamonds down the center. Use your favorite panel lap robe instruction.

Step 2 – Crocheted Foundation:

Row 1: Since our panels were knit on a machine with no tension bar, use a size G crochet hook to work one row of sc to ensure a firm base and straight edges. Place first panel on your lap, right side up. Insert hook in first st at right outside end of long side at Point 1 of Figure 6. With st on hook, insert hook into next st at Point #2 of Figure 6, sc through both and repeat down length of panel. Panels measure 49 x 5-1/4 inches. Repeat for other long side. Fasten off, work in ends and trim. Repeat for all panels. Be sure all panels have same number of crocheted base stitches. Set aside.

Step 3 – Working Diamond Tatted Insertion between Machine Knit Panels:

First half of knit insertion: Place first panel right side up. Thread JTN #3 with

3 yards yarn for cc. Working from left to right, attach cc to first sc at left on outside long side of panel by running JTN through that st (catching both sides of st), through loop of cc, and securing to that st. Ch 6 dsb, sson. R of 3 ds, 3 p sep by 3 ds, 3 ds, sson, clr. Ch 6 dsb, sson.

*Sk 2 sts on panel edge and j to next st by running JTN through st, between strands of cc, securing to edge and moving ball strand away from ch. After joining, place ball strand over JTN, then down to continue tatting.

Ch 6 dsb, sson. R of 3 ds, j to last p of previous r, 3 ds, p, 3 ds, p, 3 ds, sson, clr. Ch 6 dsb, sson. Repeat from * across panel, ending sk 2 sts and j to panel end. Repeat first half of insertion on all panels and set aside.

Second half of knit insertion: Place one panel right side up with one end near you, opposite end extends away from you with first tatted half on right. Place second panel to the right of first panel and in the same position. Tatted edge will be on the left facing a plain edge to the right; you will be working between them. Thread JTN with 3 yards of yarn for cc. Attach cc to first st nearest you in right panel, the same as for first panel.

Ch 6 dsb, sson. Instead of making a r, j to first r nearest you in left panel as follows: Place ball strand away from ch. Pick up first r of left panel nearest you, and with thumbs open middle p. Run JTN through center of r, between strands of cc, and secure on open p. Pick up ball strand and bring it back over work. Place r on JTN under right thumb, 6 dsb, sson. Sk 2 sts on edge of second panel. Move ball strand away from ch. J ch to next st in panel. Pick up ball strand and repeat from * across right panel. Remove JTN after last ch is j to last st of right panel. Work in ends with yarn needle and trim. Repeat second half of insertion to work all panels together.

Border for Lap Robe: Thread JTN with 3 yards yarn for cc. Place lap robe right side up and start in any corner. R of 3 ds, p, 3 ds, j to st at corner on right side of corner, 2 ds, p, 4 ds, sson, clr. Ch 9 dsb, sson. R of 4 ds, j to last p of previous r, 2 ds, j to first st on other side of corner, 3 ds, p, 3 ds, sson, clr. Repeat at other corners. Ch 9 dsb, sson.

*R of 3 ds, j to last p of previous r, 3 ds, sk 2 sts on edge of panel, j to next st, 3 ds, p, 3 ds, sson, clr. Ch 9 dsb, sson. Repeat from * across panel between corners. Run JTN up center of first r of first corner, between strands of cc, and secure to base of r − (rnr). Remove JTN, work in ends and trim.

By placing panels as instructed, tatted insertions can be combined with panels for afghans or garments.

ATTACHING TATTED FRINGE TO A CROCHETED OR KNIT AFGHAN AS IT IS BEING MADE

When longer picots are worked into chains and rings and remain loose, they make lovely fringe. There are three types of fringe: (1) picots worked into chains alone are simple fringe; (2) picots worked into chains of a row of rings and chains are ring and chain fringe; and (3) picots worked into rings of a row of rings and chains are called ring fringe. These fringes can be attached to a crocheted, knit or serged article as it is being made.

Simple Fringe

Knit a 30-st, 3-inch swatch by hand or machine. Working from right to left using the same yarn as swatch, thread JTN with 1-1/2 yards of yarn for cc. Attach cc to knit swatch by running JTN up through a knit st (catching two sides of the st) at right end of swatch, back through loop of cc, and securing cc to the knit st. *Ch 3 ds, 4 two-finger p, ending 3 ds, sson, clr. Sk 2 st on knit edge, run JTN through next st, between strands of cc, and secure on st. Repeat from * (see Figure 7).

Try making this trimming with longer picots. Without picots, use this chain for button loops on a garment. Since this is a chain only, it is worked from right to left. If you prefer working from left to right, remember to tat ds stitches instead of dsb stitches.

Fringe on Chains of a Row of Rings and Chains

Knit or crochet a 3-inch swatch using 30 stitches. Thread JTN with 1-1/2 yards of yarn for cc. R of 3 ds, p, 3 ds, pick up swatch with right side facing, j to first st on right end edge by inserting tip of the JTN (both sides of the st), catch ball strand with tip of JTN and pull it through swatch to form a loop. Keep loop on JTN. Tighten ball strand on JTN, 3 ds, p, 3 ds, sson, clr. *Ch 3 dsb, 4 two-finger p, 3 dsb, sson. R of 3 ds, j to last p of previous r, 3 ds, sk 2 sts on edge of swatch and j to next st, 3 ds, p, 3 ds, sson, clr. Repeat from * (see Figure 8).

The extended four-finger picots can be used for ponchos, shawls and blankets.

Fringe on the Rings of a Row of Rings and Chains

To make this fringe, tatting must be worked from left to right, because the chain is being attached to the crochet or knit piece rather than the ring.

Thread JTN with 1-1/2 yards of yarn

Fig. 7   **Fig. 8**

for cc. Attach cc to first st at left end of swatch by running JTN through st, catching both sides of st. Run JTN through loop end of cc and secure on swatch st. Ch 4 dsb, sson. R of ds, p, 2 ds, 4 two-finger p, 2 ds, p, 3 ds, sson, clr. Ch 4 dsb, sson. Sk 2 sts on swatch edge, run JTN through next st, between strands of cc, secure on st, 4 dsb, sson. *R of 3 ds, j to last p of previous r, 2 ds, 4 two-finger p, 2 ds, p, 3 ds, sson, clr. Ch 4 dsb, sson. Sk 2 sts on swatch edge, j to next st by running JTN through st, between strands of cc, and securing. Ch 4 dsb, sson. Repeat from * for desired length (see Figure 9).

Making a Different Fringe to Attach to a Row of Rings and Chains

Cut some 12-inch strands from the same yarn used for afghan. Cut a 6x3-inch piece of cardboard for winding yarn. *Fold two strands in half and with size G crochet hook, draw two loops through first ring at one end of afghan, leaving the two loops on hook, draw four ends of same strand through loops. Tighten fringe at base of ring. Repeat from * until all rings have been fringed.

ATTACHING RINGS AND CHAINS TO SERGED FABRIC

Fabrics finished with a serged edge can also be trimmed with a needle tatted edge. Remember to select tatting needle and thread compatible with fabric. When using fine tatting needles and threads with delicate fabric, the appearance will be traditional. Larger needles and threads or yarns with heavier fabrics, such as corduroy, wools, upholstery or drapery materials, will have a moderately traditional appearance.

Attaching a Needle Tatted Trim to a Serged Edge

Thread JTN #00 with 2 yards thread for cc. Working from right to left, pick up piece, insert JTN under an inverted "V" of the serging (see Figure 10). Remembering to push needle under two threads of the serging, pull JTN through and sk two inverted "V's." Continue working as simple fringe.

Attaching Rings in a Row of Rings and Chains Where Only Chains Can Be Fringed

Thread JTN with 2 yards thread for cc. R of 3 ds, p, 3 ds, j to serged edge using a #7 steel crochet hook. Insert crochet hook under inverted "V" st, catch ball strand with hook (see Figure 11). Pull hook out, placing loop from ball strand on JTN. Tighten loop from ball strand on JTN and continue working as a fringe on chains of a row of rings and chains.

Attaching Chains of a Row of Rings and Chains That May Have Fringe in Rings

Thread JTN with 2 yards thread for cc. When attaching rings and chains in this manner, it is best to work from left to right. This method is easier because work will not have to be reversed. Attach cc to serged edge by running JTN under an inverted "V" as in Figure 12. Continue working as a fringe on the rings of a row of rings and chains.

Fig. 10

Ball Strand — Outside edge

Crochet Hook

Fig. 9   Fig. 11   Fig. 12

PROJECTS

Betsy's Ponytail Holder

This instruction gives the beginner a chance to practice joining chains to chains and to a serged edge.

Materials: JTN #000 and threader, embroidery needle and scissors, 7 inches of 2-inch-wide ribbon of color desired, satin ribbon 1/2 inch wide and 20 inches long, matching sewing thread, 1/4 ball white DMC #12 thread for cc and 1/4 ball white DMC tatting thread.

Step 1 – Satin Base: Serge both ends of wider satin ribbon. Use DMC #12 for top thread on serger. Fold ribbon lengthwise (satin side out) and serge two sides together. Work in ends and trim. When not using serger, fold ends under and machine stitch. Fold lengthwise and sew sides together with a running eyelet stitch. If preferred, make tiny hand running stitches at both folded ends and sew two sides together with tiny buttonhole stitches.

Step 2 – Tatted Edging: Row 1: Thread JTN with 1-1/2 yards DMC #12 for cc. Run JTN through stitch of satin base (catch 2 threads) at left end of serged or sewn edge. Run JTN through loop of cc and secure at base. In working from left to right, chain ds only (not dsb). Ch 8 ds, p, 8 ds, sson. *Move 1/2 inch to right on satin base, run JTN through two st (catch 2 threads), between two strands of cc, and secure to edge. Repeat from * across base. Remove JTN, sew in ends and trim.

Row 2: Thread JTN with 2 yards DMC #12 for cc. Run JTN through same st where first ch was attached in previous row, back through loop of cc, and secure at base. With DMC #8, ch 16 ds, sson. R of 5 ds, p, 10 ds, p, 5 ds, sson, clr. *Ch 8 ds, sson. Run JTN through p of first ch of previous row, between strands of cc, and secure on p. Ch 8 ds, sson. R of

5 ds, j to last p of previous r, 10 ds, p, 5 ds, sson, clr. Repeat from *, moving to next p in next ch of previous row until all ch and last r are made, ending with 16 ds, sson. Run JTN through same st where last ch of previous row was connected, between strands of cc, and secure on st. Remove JTN, sew in ends and trim.

Row 3: Thread JTN with 1-1/2 yards DMC #12 for cc. Run JTN up first p of first r at left base, back through loop of cc, and secure to p. With DMC #8, *ch 3 ds, 5 p sep by 2 ds, 3 ds, sson. Run JTN through p connecting first and second r, through strands of cc, and secure to p. Repeat from * across all r, moving over one r each time a ch is completed. Attach last ch to last p of last r. Remove JTN, sew in ends and trim.

Step 3: Weave narrow ribbon through base, even ends and tack ribbon with needle and thread, taking a few back stitches to hold in place. To wear, push each end to center, gathering base, and tie to ponytail with a bow.

Add needle tatting to embroidery, needlepoint and quilting or use needle tatting motifs as appliqué. Daisies made of DMC #8 and a JTN #00 can be appliquéd to yokes of dresses, blouses or household items.

Oval Place Mat with Tatted Appliqué and Border

Materials: JTN #00 and threader, embroidery needle and scissors. Oval place mat patterns are available at your local fabric store or you can purchase ready-made place mats. For 6 place mats use 6 skeins pink DMC #5, 1/4 ball green DMC #5, 2 skeins pink DMC #8, needle and white sewing thread, 1/2 ball white DMC #8 to use on serger for top threads, size 7 crochet hook.

Step 1: Stitch quilted place mats from your favorite pattern. Serge place mats with DMC #8 for the top threads. Use regular thread for the other needles to stitch down top threads, work in ends and trim.

Step 2: Thread JTN with 3 yards pink DMC #8 for cc and DMC #5 for tatting. R of 3 ds, p, 3 ds, with crochet hook j to an inverted "V" in serged edge (see Figure 10). Ch 3 ds, p, 3 ds, sson, clr. Ch 9 dsb, sson. *Ch 3 ds, j to last p of previous r, 3 ds, sk two inverted "V's" on serged edge. With hook, j to next inverted "V," 3 ds, p, 3 ds, sson, clr. Ch 9 dsb, sson. Repeat from * around place mat to last 5 inverted "V's." R of 3 ds, j to last p of previous r, 3 ds, with hook sk 2 inverted "V's" in serged edge and j to next inverted "V." Ch 3 ds, j to first p of first r, 3 ds, sson, clr. Ch 9 dsb, sson. Run JTN up center of first r, between strands of cc, and secure to base of first r (rnr). Remove JTN, work in ends and trim.

Step 3 – Large Center Flower: Thread JTN with 1-1/2 yards pink DMC #8 for cc. With green, r of 2 ds, 7 p sep by 2 ds, 2 ds, sson, clr. Cut thread, work in ends and trim. The petals of this flower are made with mock rings (see Chapter III).

With pink DMC #5, ch petals by working around center r clockwise. Ch 3 ds, p, 6 ds, p, 6 ds, p, 3 ds, sson. Run JTN up p to right of ch of r. Be sure right side of r is facing. Run JTN between strands of cc and secure ch on p (rnr). *Ch 3 ds, j to first p of previous mock ring or petal, 6 ds, p, 6 ds, p, 3 ds, sson. J to next p of center r, rnr and secure ch on p. Repeat from * 5 times. Ch 3 ds, j to last p of previous petal, 6 ds, p, 6 ds, pull first petal around with left hand as if to clasp a necklace. J to first p, ch 3 ds, sson. Remove JTN, sew in ends and trim.

Step 4 – Small Side Flowers and Stems: Thread JTN with 1-1/2 yards pink DMC #8 for cc. With DMC #5, r of 9 ds, p, 6 ds, p, 3 ds, sson, clr. Ch 1 ds, sson. R of 3 ds, j to last p of previous

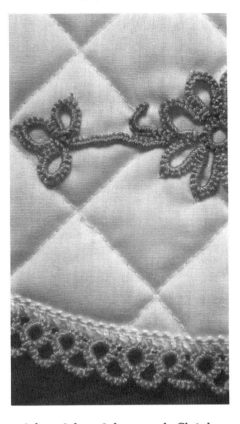

r, 6 ds, p, 6 ds, p, 3 ds, sson, clr. Ch 1 ds, sson. R of 3 ds, j to last p of previous r, 6 ds, p, 6 ds, p, 9 ds, sson, clr. Cut thread, work in ends. With green, ch 16 ds, p, 6 ds, sson. Run JTN through p between any two petals of large flower, between strands of cc, and secure to p. Ch 6 ds, j to last p of stem. Ch 10 ds, sson. Remove JTN, work in ends. Repeat this step for small flower and stem on opposite side.

Step 5 – Appliqué Tatted Flower: Pin flower as shown and use white thread for small running backstitches to catch only the lower ridge of double stitches around large and small flowers and stems. Place mats can be machine washed, but it is best to lay flat for drying. Press lightly if desired.

CONVERTING SHUTTLE PATTERNS TO JIFFY NEEDLE TATTING

Five major points must be considered when converting shuttle patterns to Jiffy Needle Tatting. The pearl bead collar shown with 19 points was tatted using the traditional ball and shuttle method. The pearl bead collar shown with 13 points was tatted using the Jiffy Tatting Needle. Refer to the pictures of these collars and pattern instructions for each when considering the following five points:

1. The pattern must be a ball and shuttle pattern. Some shuttle-only patterns can be adapted if the thread between rings is short.

2. The position of the rings is important. The collar has two rows, each composed of groups of rings into motifs. The upper row shows groups of five rings and the lower row shows groups of four rings.

3. It is important to understand how chains are used to link rings together and just where some chains are linked to other chains. When looking at ball and shuttle patterns, always examine them from left to right.

Start with the lower second motif from left end of collar and trace the chains around. Continue tracing chains up to and along the right two rings of the upper group. Notice the line makes a sharp turn to the right twice, down the left side of the next upper group of rings. As you continue in this way you will soon identify how the rings were grouped together in the motif by the chains and also how each motif was joined to the other motif.

Notice that the 5th ring in the upper group of rings was added to the group of four upper rings after the top row was complete. The upper and lower groups of rings were done in two stages. The upper left two rings were done first, fol-

lowed by the lower left two rings. After the beaded point at the bottom, the chain moves up the two lower right rings (see Figure 1); it continues the upper right ring. It then turns sharply to the right and back down the left side of the next upper and lower rings and continues until the double row is completed. It is important to follow the pattern until you understand how chains link up with rings.

4. If beads are used, the method used to work them into the project needs to be determined. Compare how beads appear in the shuttle tatted collar to how they appear in methods shown in Chapter IV. Since the collar has beads in it, the next thing to do is to take note of the size of the beads used and try to determine how they were worked into the collar (whether from the ball strand or worked with the picot). Notice the double motif columns of each collar. There are 19 double motifs in the shuttle tatted collar, 13 double motifs in the Jiffy Needle tatted collar.

5. The thread used is important. Most

Fig. 1

times shuttle patterns are worked with fine tatting thread or crochet thread. Usually crochet thread has a "hard" or "tight" twist. Crochet thread is not the best type to use with the tatting needle.

Look for threads with a soft twist such as DMC pearl cotton. The shuttle pattern calls for #30 crochet thread. It has a hard twist, and so DMC #5 and #8 were selected to get a softer twist.

PROJECT

Shuttle Pearl Beaded Collar

(The following pattern is from the book TATTING PATTERNS by the staff of WORKBASKET Magazine)

Note: Shuttle tatting abbreviations are the same as Jiffy Needle Tatting except close ring is written cl r. An additional abbreviation used is rw, meaning reverse work.

Materials: 95 yards #30 crochet cotton, 60-inch string of 3mm pearl beads, beading needle, tatting shuttle and size 13 steel crochet hook for joining picots. String 171 beads on ball thread.

Point Scallop: R of 6 ds, p, 6 ds, cl r, rw. With ball and shuttle threads, ch 5 ds, 4 p sep by 2 ds, 5 ds, rw. *R of 6 ds, join in p of last r, 6 ds, cl r, rw. Place bead. Ch 4 ds, p, 4 ds, rw. R of 6 ds, p, 6 ds, cl r, rw. Place bead. Ch 5 ds, 4 p sep by 2 ds, 5 ds, rw. R of 6 ds, join in p of last r, 6 ds, cl r, rw. Place bead. Ch 5 ds, p, 3 ds, place 3 beads, 3 ds, p, 5 ds, rw. R of 6 ds, join between two joined r's, 6 ds, cl r, rw. Place bead. Ch 5 ds, 4 p sep by 2 ds, 5 ds, rw. R of 6 ds, join in same place with last r, 6 ds, cl r, rw. Place bead. Ch 4 ds, p, 4 ds, rw. R of 6 ds, join between two joined r's, 6 ds, cl r, rw. Place bead. Ch 5 ds, 4 p sep by 2 ds, 5 ds, rw. R of 6 ds, join in same place with last r, 6 ds, cl r, rw. Ch 5 ds, p, 5 ds, rw. R of 6 ds, p, 6 ds, cl r, rw. Ch 5 ds, p, 2 ds, sk 1 p of adjacent ch, join in next p, 2 ds, join in next p of same ch, 2 ds, p, 5 ds, rw. Repeat from * for length desired. Tie and cut threads.

Neck Edge: R of 6 ds, join in joining of 4 r's at beginning, 6 ds, cl r, rw. *Ch 5 ds, p, 5 ds, rw. R of 3 ds, join in p of next ch, 3 ds, cl r, rw. Ch 5 ds, p, 5 ds, rw. R of 6 ds, join in next joining of 4 r's, 6 ds, cl r, rw. Repeat from * across collar. Tie and cut threads.

Joined Rings Between Points: R of 3 ds, join in first p of 4-p-ch (p nearest tip of point), 3 ds, cl r. R of 3 ds, join in corresponding p of next point, 3 ds, cl r. Tie and cut threads. Repeat between each point across collar.

If pressing is needed, place on folded Turkish towel and carefully press under a folded, damp cloth.

Pearl Beaded Collar Converted to Jiffy Needle Tatting

Materials: JTN #00, threader, embroidery needle, 6 inches of wire to string beads, scissors, ball of DMC #8 for carrying cord, ball of DMC #5 for tatting, 113 size 4mm pearl beads, size 7

crochet hook, 3/4x 3-inch cardboard.

Cover work area with a dark cloth for contrast while working with white threads and beads. Beads can be easily lost and the cloth helps to reduce their tendency to roll.

Fold 6-inch bead wire in half, thread with DMC #5, string 89 beads and push them down into the ball. Use a bead threader from craft shop if desired. Reserve remaining 24 beads for long picots; each is worked individually later. Thread JTN with 3 yards of DMC #8 for cc.

First Left Half Upper Motif in First Column – Left End Of Collar: R of 6 ds, p, 6 ds, sson, clr. Ch 5 dsb, 3 p sep by 2 dsb, 5 dsb, sson. R of 6 ds, j to p of previous r, 6 ds, sson, clr.

Bridge Chain Between Motifs: Ch 4 dsb, slide bead to JTN, 4 dsb, sson.

First Lower Left Half of Motif: Repeat instructions for first column. *Ch 5 dsb, p, 3 dsb, slide 3 beads to JTN, 3 dsb, p, 5 dsb, sson. Use left thumb and index finger to push ds with beads off JTN. (Beads divide the straight row of double stitches and can be difficult to get off. Keep ds close together when sliding off JTN).

R of 6 ds, j to p where no previous r are connected, 6 ds, sson, clr. Ch 5 dsb, p, 2 dsb, p, 2 dsb, 1 measured picot (mp). Place cardboard next to dsb st under JTN, 2 dsb, remove cardboard, p, 2 dsb, p, 5 dsb, sson (see Figure 1 and note measured picot). R of 6 ds, j to p where 3 previous r are connected, 6 ds, sson, clr. Repeat bridge chain.

Second Half of Upper Motif: R of 6 ds, j to p connecting two r of first upper half of motif, 6 ds, sson, clr. Ch 5 dsb, p, 2 dsb, p, 2 dsb, slide 2 beads, 2 dsb, p, 5 dsb, sson. R of 6 ds, j to same p where 3 r are connected in upper motif. Ch 6 ds, sson, clr. Ch 5 ds, p, 5 ds, sson (this ch is made with ds because it stands and does not turn down), cross to right for position to work second motif column.

First Half Upper Motif of Second Column: R of 6 ds, p, 6 ds, sson, clr. Turn work clockwise and place on table. Pass cc under ball strand toward you; cc is drawn across top. The tip of scallop points at left are away from you. Ch 5 dsb, p, 2 dsb, j to second p between two beads in ch at left, 2 dsb, p, 2 dsb, p, 5 dsb, sson. Turn work counterclockwise, moving cc to back. R of 6 ds, j to p of previous r, 6 ds, sson, clr. Repeat bridge chain between motifs only.

First Half Lower Motif of Second Column: R of 6 ds, p, 6 ds, sson, clr. Turn work clockwise. Bring cc toward you under ball strand. Ch 5 dsb, p, 2 dsb, lay JTN down. Pick up wire, insert it on long picot (lp); mp is in opposite ch at left in previous lower motif. String two beads on wire, leaving wire on p. Insert crochet hook in p next to wire; avoid splitting thread. Pull ball strand through to form a loop. Place loop on JTN and remove wire. Give ball strand a tug to tighten beaded p. Ch 2 dsb, p, 2 dsb, p, 5 dsb, sson.

Turn work counterclockwise. Move cc to back of work. R of 6 ds, j to p of previous r, 6 ds, clr, sson. Repeat from * 11 times. Do not work last two sets of lower and upper right rings, but work mp fingertip p. Ch 6 ds, j to last p where 2 previous r are connected, 6 ds, sson, clr. Ch 5 dsb, 4 p sep by 2 dsb, 5 dsb, sson. R of 5 ds, j to last p connecting previous 3 r, 6 ds, sson, clr. Ch 4 ds, slide bead, 4 dsb, sson. R of 6 ds, j to p connecting 2 upper r, 6 ds, sson, clr. Ch 5 dsb, 4 p sep by 2 dsb, 5 dsb, sson. R of 6 ds, j to same p where previous r was connected, 6 ds, sson, clr. Do not cut cc or ball strand.

Neck Row: Thread JTN with 3 yards DMC #8 for cc. Ch 5 dsb, p, 5 dsb, sson. R of 6 ds, j to p in upper motif of first column at right end of collar where 4 r are connected, 6 ds, sson, clr. Ch 5 dsb, p, 5 dsb, sson. R of 3 ds, j to p in crossover ch between upper motifs, 3 ds, sson, clr. Ch 5 dsb, p, 5 dsb, sson. R of 6 ds, j to p in upper motif of next column. Ch 6 ds, sson, clr. Repeat all columns, ending ch 5 dsb, p, 5 dsb, sson. Run JTN up last r of last motif, between strands of cc, and secure on r. Remove JTN, work in ends and trim.

Turn collar right side down on white towel. To block, spray starch on wet sponge and pat collar. Place white cloth over collar, press lightly.

READY, SET, TAT! HOLIDAY PATTERNS

Aren't you proud of yourself?! You've learned the basic techniques of Jiffy Needle Tatting and you're a "pro" at working the practice instructions. Now select your favorite patterns from this collection, and get ready, set, tat!

Imagine the astonished but appreciative comments when family and friends receive beautiful, unusual gifts made with your newfound talent – Jiffy Needle Tatting!

Tat the beaded tree for Dad's office or den and the satin ornaments for Mother. Just imagine how delighted Aunt Sophie will be when she decorates her home with snowflakes. The note paper makes a great gift for Susan when she's away at school.

All these holiday patterns make great gifts or make them for yourself to add a festive touch in your own home!

Christmas Tree Wall Hanging

Tree measures approximately 6 x 11 inches.

Materials: JTN #3 or #4 and threader, yarn needle and scissors, small size crochet hook for beads, 1 ounce green 4-ply yarn, six 6mm x 9mm red Pony beads, five 2mm x 9mm silver Pony beads.

Row 1: Thread JTN with 2 yards yarn for cc. Work from the bottom up. R of 4 ds, 3 p sep by 4 ds, 4 ds, sson, clr. *Ch 6 dsb, p, 6 dsb, sson. R of 4 ds. Hold JTN with little finger of right hand, freeing thumb and index fingers for crochet hook. Insert hook into red bead and pull last p of previous r through bead, retaining p on hook. With hook, draw loop from ball strand through p and loop on JTN. Do this each time the direction is given to bead a picot, abbreviated as bp. As you bp, alternate the color of the bead, continue with 4 ds, p, 4 ds, p, 4 ds, sson, clr. *Ch 6 dsb, p, 6 dsb, sson. R of 4 ds, j to last p of previous r, 4 ds, p, 4 ds, p, 4 ds, sson, clr. Repeat from * once.

Ch 6 dsb, p, 6 dsb, sson. R of 4 ds, bp and j to last p of previous r, 4 ds, p, 4 ds, p, 4 ds, sson, clr. Ch 6 dsb, p, 6 dsb, sson. R of 4 ds, j to last p of previous r, 4 ds, p, 4 ds, p, 4 ds, sson, clr. Ch 6 dsb, p, 6 dsb, sson. R of 4 ds, bp and j to last p of previous r, 4 ds, p, 4 ds, p, 4 ds, sson, clr – 7 rings. Remove JTN, work in ends and trim.

Row 2: Thread JTN with 2 yards yarn for cc. R of 4 ds, p, 4 ds, j to p of first ch of previous row, 4 ds, p, 4 ds, sson, clr. Ch 6 dsb, p, 6 dsb, sson. R of 4 ds, bp and j to p of previous r, 4 ds, j to p of 2nd ch of previous row, 4 ds, p, 4 ds, sson, clr. Ch 6 dsb, p, 6 dsb, sson.

R of 4 ds, j to last p of previous r, 4 ds, j to p in next ch of previous row, 4 ds, p, 4 ds, sson, clr. Ch 6 dsb, p, 6 dsb, sson. R of 4 ds, bp and j to last p of previous r, 4 ds, j to p in next ch of previous row, 4 ds, p, 4 ds, sson, clr. Ch 6 dsb, p, 6 dsb, sson. R of 4 ds, j to last p of previous r, 4 ds, j to p in next ch of previous row, 4 ds, p, 4 ds, sson, clr. Ch 6 dsb, p, 6 dsb, sson. R of 4 ds, bp and j to last p of previous r, 4 ds, j to p in last ch of previous row, 4 ds, p, 4 ds, sson, clr. Remove JTN, work in ends and trim.

Row 3: Thread JTN with 1-1/2 yards yarn for cc. Repeat Row 2 except bp with red beads to last p of previous first and 4th r.

Row 4: Thread JTN with 1-1/2 yards yarn for cc. Repeat Row 2 except bp with silver bead to last p of 2nd r.

Row 5: Thread JTN with 1 yard yarn for cc. Repeat Row 2 except bp with red bead to last p of 2nd r.

Row 6: Thread JTN with 1 yard yarn for cc. R of 4 ds, p, 4 ds, j to p in first ch of previous row, 4 ds, p, 4 ds, sson, clr. Ch 6 dsb, sson. R of 4 ds, 3 p sep by 4 ds, 4 ds, sson, clr. Ch 6 dsb, sson. R of 4 ds, bp with silver bead to last p of previous r, 4 ds, j to p in next ch of previous row, 4 ds, p, 4 ds, sson, clr. Remove JTN, work in ends and trim.

Base of Tree: Thread JTN with 1 yard yarn for cc. Turn tree upside down. Run JTN through p, connecting 3rd and 4th r from right in first row, through loop of

cc to secure cc to p (rnp). Ch 10 dsb, sson. R of 4 ds, j to p on r at left, 4 ds, tp, 8 ds, sson, clr. Ch 12 dsb, sson.

With thumbs, open ds at tp in previous r. Run JTN through center of r, between strands of cc. Turn tree so top points left. Secure ch over tp by tugging cc to tighten ch to the r, ending with 10 dsb, sson. J to p between 3rd and 4th r from left in first row, rnp. Remove JTN, sew ends and trim.

Note: This tree can be made with any size JTN, beads and yarn. By adding rings to the first row, the tree will be longer.

Joy's Angel Kewpie Doll Outfit

Materials: JTN #0 and threader, yarn needle and scissors, needle-nose pliers, 8-inch cupie doll, 2 ounces DMC #3 pearl cotton, 18 inches red 1/2-inch ribbon, 13 inches 18-gauge cloth covered wire, 4x20-inch piece blue satin for half slip, sewing needle and thread, straight pins.

Gauge: Use tiny picots (tp) 1/4 inch wide throughout this pattern.

Yoke: Thread JTN with 1-3/4 yards DMC #3 for cc. R of 6 ds, 3 p sep by 3 ds, 3 ds, sson, clr. Ch 3 dsb, p, 3 dsb, p, 3 dsb, sson. R of 3 ds, j to last p of previous r, 3 ds, p, 3 ds, p, 3 ds, sson, clr — right back yoke complete. Ch 3 dsb, 4 p sep by 3 dsb, 3 dsb, sson — right underarm ch complete. R of 3 ds, 3 p sep by 3 ds, 3 ds, sson, clr.

*Ch 3 dsb, p, 3 dsb, p, 3 dsb, sson. R of 3 ds, j to last p of previous r, 3 ds, p, 3 ds, p, 3 ds, sson, clr, sson. Repeat from * twice — front yoke complete. Ch 3 dsb, 4 p sep by 3 dsb, 3 dsb, sson — left underarm ch complete. R of 3 ds, 3 p sep by 3 ds, 3 ds, sson, clr. Ch 3 dsb, p, 3 dsb, p, 3 dsb, sson. R of 3 ds, j to last p of previous r, 3 ds, p, 6 ds, sson, clr — left yoke complete. Remove JTN, sew ends into base of r and trim (see Figure 1).

Skirt: Rnd 1: Thread JTN with 2-1/2 yards DMC #8 for cc (piece cc as needed). R of 6 ds, j to first p of first ch in previous rnd (see Figure 1 at arrow — upper p, right back yoke), 3 ds, p, 3 ds, sson, clr. Ch 4 dsb, p, 4 dsb, sson. R of 3 ds, j to last p of previous r, 3 ds, j to same p in yoke, 3 ds, p, 3 ds, sson, clr — 2 r connected to 1 p. Ch 4 dsb, p, 4 dsb, sson. R of 3 ds, j to last p of previous r, 3 ds, j to next p in same ch of yoke, 3 ds, p, 3 ds, sson, clr. Ch 4 dsb, p, 4 dsb, sson. R of 3 ds, j to last p of previous r, 3 ds, j to same p in first ch of yoke, 3 ds, p, 3 ds, sson, clr. Repeat, making 2 r in every p of each ch in yoke — 35 r sep by

ch of 4 dsb, p, 4 dsb, sson. Ch 4 dsb, p, 4 dsb, sson. R of 3 ds, j to p in previous r, 3 ds, j to same p in yoke, 6 ds, sson, clr. Do not cut cc. Ch 4 dsb, p, 4 dsb, sson. Run JTN up center of r at beginning of rnd, between strands of cc, and secure ch to base of r, rnr. Remove JTN, work ends into base of r and trim.

Rnd 2: Thread JTN with 2-1/2 yards of DMC #3 for cc. R of 3 ds, p, 3 ds, j to p in any ch of previous rnd, 3 ds, p, 3 ds, sson, clr.

*Ch 4 dsb, p, 4 dsb, sson. R of 3 ds, j to last p of previous r, 3 ds, j to p in next ch of previous rnd, 3 ds, p, 3 ds, sson, clr. Repeat from * 33 times, ch 4 dsb, p, 4 dsb, sson. R of 3 ds, j to last p of previous r, 3 ds, j to p in next ch of previous rnd, 3 ds, j to first p in first r at beginning of rnd, 3 ds, sson, clr. Ch 4 dsb, p, 4 dsb, sson. J to base of first r, rnr. Remove JTN, work ends into base of first r and trim.

Rnd 3: Repeat Rnd 2.

Rnd 4 — Hem Round: Thread JTN with 2-1/2 yards DMC #3 for cc. R of 6 ds, p, 3 ds, j to p in any ch of previous rnd, 3 ds, sson, clr. Ch 4 ds (do not dsb for this ch), j to p in next ch of previous rnd, sson. R of 3 ds, j to p in next ch of previous rnd, 3 ds, p, 6 ds, sson, clr. Ch 3 dsb, 9 dsb, sson. J to last p of previous r, rnp.

*Ch 9 dsb, p, 3 dsb, sson, clr. R of 6 ds, j to p where previous ch and r are connected, 3 ds, j to p in next ch in previous rnd, 3 ds, sson, clr. *Ch 4 ds, j to p in next ch of previous rnd, 4 ds, sson. R of 3 ds, j to p in next ch of previous rnd, 3 ds, p, 6 ds, sson, clr. Turn work clockwise, bringing cc toward you, under ball strand and across previous r. Ch 3 dsb, j to p in ch at left, 9 dsb, sson.

Turn work counterclockwise, drawing cc to back of work, j to last p of previous r, rnp. Repeat from * 10 times. Ch 9 dsb, fold back first ch at beginning of rnd, j to p of that ch, 3 dsb, sson. J to base of first r at beginning of rnd, rnr. Remove JTN, work in ends and trim.

Neckline Rnd: Thread JTN with 1 yard DMC #3 for cc. Attach cc to dress by running JTN through middle p in first r of left back yoke, through loop of cc, and secure cc on p (avoid pulling p). Ch 8 dsb, sson. J to middle p of next r of left yoke, rnp — left back yoke neck complete, ch 4 ds (do not dsb), p, 4 ds, p, 4 ds, sson (avoid bunching ds) — left shoulder strap complete. J to middle p on next r of front yoke, rnp.

*Ch 8 dsb, sson, j to middle p in next r, rnp. Repeat from * twice — front yoke neck completed. Ch 4 ds (do not dsb), p, 4 ds, p, 4 ds, sson — right shoulder strap (avoid bunching ds). J to middle p of

Fig. 1

Right Wing

Fig. 2

next r of right back yoke, rnp. Ch 8 dsb, sson. Rnp in middle p of last r of yoke. Remove JTN, work ends into ch and trim.

Left Shoulder Ruffle: Thread JTN with 2 yards DMC #3 for cc. See Figure 1 to start left sleeve ruffle. With yoke front facing and hem skirt at right, attach cc to first p at front of underarm ch where two r of first row are attached. Run JTN through p, through loop of cc, and secure on p.

R of 6 ds, j to free p in left r of front yoke, 3 ds, p, 3 ds, sson, clr. Ch 10 dsb, sson. R of 3 ds, j to last p of previous r, 3 ds, j to same p in left r of front yoke, 3 ds, p, 3 ds, sson, clr. Ch 10 dsb, sson. R of 3 ds, j to last p of previous r, 3 ds, j to first p in left shoulder strap, 3 ds, p, 3 ds, sson, clr. Ch 10 dsb, sson.

R of 3 ds, j to last p of previous r, 3 ds, j to same p in shoulder strap, 3 ds, p, 3 ds, sson, clr. Ch 10 dsb, sson. R of 3 ds, j to last p of previous r, 3 ds, j to next p in shoulder strap, 3 ds, p, 3 ds, sson, clr. Ch 10 dsb, sson. R of 3 ds, j to last p of previous r, 3 ds, j to same p in shoulder strap, 3 ds, p, 3 ds, sson, clr. Ch 10 dsb, sson.

R of 3 ds, j to last p of previous r, 3 ds, j to free p in r of back left yoke, 3 ds, p, 3 ds, sson, clr. Ch 10 dsb, sson. R of 3 ds, j to last p of previous r, 3 ds, j to same p of back left yoke, 6 ds, sson, clr. Remove JTN, working ends around right inside p of ch of left underarm, back into r and trim. Repeat for ruffle on right shoulder strap.

Wings: The center ring holding the two wings is worked with dsb knots to ensure that all work will be on the right side. Thread JTN with 3 yards yarn for cc.

Center Ring: R of 2 dsb, 9 p sep by 2 dsb, 2 dsb, sson, clr. **Ch 10 ds, sson. R of 4 ds, p, 8 ds, p, 4 ds, sson, clr – first outer ring. Ch 10 dsb, sson. Working clockwise around center r, j to center r by turning with right side (knot side) facing; tail is at left. Avoid twist to tat-

ted ch and r. J to first p at right of previous ch, rnp.

Ch 10 ds, sson. R of 4 ds, j to last p of previous outer r, 8 ds, p, 4 ds, sson, clr. Ch 10 dsb, sson. J to next p in center r, rnp. Repeat from ** 3 times except j last ch to center r as follows: Open p with thumbs, j to open p by running JTN up center of r, between strands of cc, and secure on open p – first wing complete (see Figure 2). Repeat from ** to complete the second wing. Attach last ch to base of center r, rnr. Remove JTN, work in ends and trim.

Border Chain for Wings: Thread JTN with 1 yard DMC #3 for cc. Attach cc to p in first r on right side of one wing (right side facing) by running JTN up p, through loop of cc, and securing cc on p.

*Ch 12 dsb, sson. J to p between first and second r, rnp. Repeat from * across all outer r. Remove JTN, work in ends and trim. Repeat Border Chain for other wing.

Crown: Cover 10-inch piece of 18-gauge cloth-covered wire with ds. To hold ds in place, curl wire ends with pliers. Shape wire in a circle and make the first half of a square knot with the covered ends of the wire to help hold the shape. Press ends of wire down so when placed on the head, ends will hang at back of head.

Thread JTN with 1 yard thread for cc. Working counterclockwise around crown, attach cc to crown by running JTN between ds from inside the crown, through loop of cc, and securing to base. *Ch 9 dsb, sson. Move 1/2 inch to left, run JTN between ds and strands of cc to secure. Repeat from * around crown. Remove JTN, work in ends and trim.

Slip: Use stretch satin fabric for slip and diaper. Cut fabric 20 x 4-1/2 inches for slip. Hem one long side and sew two ends together. Sew top edge to form a casing for 7-inch piece of elastic. Position slip on doll under the arms.

Tie wings to top back rings of yoke with ribbon, making a bow between the wings.

Candy Cane Ornament

Materials: JTN #4 and threader, yarn needle and scissors, needle-nose pliers, 4 yards each red and white 4-ply yarn, a piece of cloth-covered 18-gauge wire.

Double red yarn and attach to wire with a Lark's Head Knot; double white yarn and attach to wire with a Lark's Head Knot next to red yarn. *Pull white double strand over red strand, tucking it between thumb and second finger of right hand. Tat 1 ds with red double strand on the wire.

Loosen white double strand from fingers of right hand and pull red over white, holding it between fingers of right hand. Tat 1 ds with white double strand and repeat from * until wire is covered. Slide ds down on wire end, making room for more ds. With pliers, bend both ends of wire back 1/2 inch over last 2 ds with needle-nose pliers and crimp to hold ds in place. Sew in ends. Shape end of wire to form candy cane. Cut 1 yard of red, double it and tie a bow on candy cane.

Note: Smaller candy cane ornaments can be made by using chenille stems. Insert the end of the stem into the eye of a JTN #4, using only 2 yards of yarn. Tat in the same manner, sliding stitch from JTN to chenille stem. Fold the ends back to secure the ds. Shape into a candy cane and tie bow.

Golden Filigree Christmas Ornament

Materials: JTN #00 and threader, tapestry needle and scissors, 6-inch piece of bead wire for threader, a toothpick, 6 yards gold DMC #8 pearl cotton for cc, 1/2 ounce gold metallic thread, twelve 6mm white pearls, twelve 2.5mm white pearls, 18 straight pins, one 3-inch diameter white satin ball.

Using the bead threader or a piece of wire, string six 6mm pearl beads onto the ball strand and push them into the ball.

Clover Round: Thread JTN with 3 yards DMC #8 for cc. *R of 4 ds, p, 4 ds, s-1b, 2 ds, p, 6 ds, sson, clr. Ch 12 dsb, sson. R of 5 ds, j to last p in previous r, 2 ds, j to right side of bead in bp of previous r, 2 ds, p, 5 ds, sson, clr.

Since the next ring is upside down, work as follows: R of 7 dsb, p, 7 dsb, sson, clr. Turn r counterclockwise so p points toward you. Bring ball strand across top of work and leave cc across back of work. Ch 12 dsb, sson. R of 6 ds, j to last p of previous r in clover, 2 ds, j to right side of bp where other two clover rings are connected, 4 ds, p, 4 ds, sson, clr. Repeat from * 5 times. Remove JTN, sew ends into base of first r at beginning of the band and trim.

Tatted Chain Rnd above the Clover Band: *Thread JTN with 18 inches DMC #8 for cc. Attach cc to the right p between any 2 pearls in the clover band by running JTN through p, through loop of cc, and securing on p.

String twelve 2-1/2mm pearl beads onto the ball strand. Leave remaining 6mm beads on ball strand.

Ch 12 dsb, s-2b, 12 dsb, sson. J ch to left p between the same 2 pearl beads in the clover band, rnp. Remove JTN, work in ends and trim. Repeat from * 5 times, each time moving to the right to j to the next 2 p in the clover band.

Beaded Ring for Bottom of Ornament: Thread JTN with 15 inches DMC #8 for cc. R of 1 ds, 6 bp (s-1b each time) sep by 2 ds, 1 ds, sson, clr. Remove JTN, sew ends into r by first skipping 1 ds to avoid unraveling the work, and trim.

Pin the clover band around the center of the satin ball. Turn ball upside down. Insert toothpick into the bottom of ball. Slip the bottom beaded ring over the toothpick. Thread tapestry needle with 1 yard metallic thread. Attach other end to bottom ring with a backstitch to the left side in any bp, *catch p in bottom r of clover band, catch right side of same bp in bottom r with backstitch, then backstitch in left side of next bp to the right in the bottom r and repeat from * until all p are worked. Sew ends into r and trim.

Turn ball upright. Thread tapestry needle with 18 inches metallic thread. Weave needle between the beads in every p in the tatted ch. Draw bp together around stem of satin ball. Wrap ends around stem to cover and take several stitches to secure work. Shape stem in a loop and add gold ties.

Morning Glory Christmas Ornament

Start by making the circle of motifs which is slipped onto the ball later.

Materials: JTN #00 and threader, tapestry needle and scissors, 1/4 ball white DMC #5 pearl cotton, 8 yards white DMC #8 pearl cotton, 73 pearl 4mm beads, 3 pearl 10mm beads, bead threader, 3-inch diameter pink satin ball, 1 toothpick, straight pins.

Using the bead threader, string 32 pearl 4mm beads onto DMC #5 thread and push them into the ball.

First Motif: Thread JTN with 39 inches DMC #8 for cc. R of 8 ds, s-1b, 2 ds, s-1b, 8 ds, sson, clr. Ch 12 dsb, s-1b, 12 dsb, sson. *R of 8 ds, j to right bead in last p in previous r, 2 ds, s-1b, 8 ds, sson, clr. Ch 12 dsb, s-1b, 12 dsb, sson. Repeat from * once. R of 8 ds, j to right of bead in last p of previous r, 2 ds, j to left of bead in first p of first r, 8 ds, sson, clr. Ch 12 dsb, s-1b, 12 dsb, sson, j ch to base of first r, rnr. Remove JTN, work in ends and trim. Set aside.

Second Motif: Thread JTN with 39 inches DMC #8 for cc. R of 8 ds, s-1b, 2 ds, s-1b, 8 ds, sson, clr. Ch 12 dsb, s-1b, 12 dsb, sson. R of 8 ds, j to right of bead in last p of previous r, 2 ds, s-1b, 8 ds, sson, clr. Ch 12 dsb. With back of previous motif facing, j to bp in any ch by inserting needle back under bead and drawing ball strand across bp. With tip of JTN, pull a loop from strand as if to knit, leaving loop on JTN. With JTN in groove between ch and bp, give ball strand a tug to tighten bp and ch together. Ch 12 dsb, sson.

R of 8 ds, j to right of bead in last p of previous r in second motif, 2 ds, s-1b, 8 ds, sson, clr. Ch 12 dsb, s-1b, 12 dsb, sson. R of 8 ds, j to left of bead in last p of previous r, 2 ds, j to left of bead in first p of first r, 8 ds, sson, clr. Ch 12 dsb, s-1b, 12 dsb, sson, j ch to base of first r,

rnr. Remove JTN, work in ends and trim.

Third Motif: Repeat 2nd motif. Set aside.

Fourth Motif: Repeat 2nd motif until you reach the last ch of the motif, ch 12 dsb. Place first motif back to back to JTN, avoiding twist in motifs. J to bp in middle ch of first motif in same manner as second motif to j the previous ch. Ch 12 dsb, sson. J ch to base of first r, rnr. Remove JTN, work in ends and trim.

Top Round of Chains and Stem Ring: Thread JTN with 1 yard DMC #8 for cc. J cc to the left side of a bp in any top ch of any motif. (Be sure back side of motif is on the outside of the circle.) J by running JTN through that p, through loop of cc, and securing to p.

*Ch 12 dsb, s-1b, 12 dsb, sson. J to bp in ch of next motif to left by inserting JTN under bead from back as instructed in 2nd motif, ch 12 dsb, sson. Repeat from * 3 times. Remove JTN, work in ends and trim.

Top Stem Ring: Thread JTN with 24 inches DMC #8 for cc. R of 2 ds, j to bp of any top ch as in second motif, except right side of work is facing, insert JTN from back, drawing ball strand across bp. Draw loop out as if to purl a stitch. *Ch 4 ds, j to bp in next ch. Repeat from * twice, 2 ds. Run JTN through loop of cc, sson, clr. Remove JTN, work in ends and trim.

Slip tatting over satin ball by working the top stem of the ball up through the top stem ring. Gently stretch the motifs down around the ball. Tip ball upside down and brace when working on bottom.

Repeat Top Round of Chains and Stem Ring to work bottom chains and center ring, leaving beads out of p in bottom ch. To make center r, place loop of cc over toothpick inserted in bottom of ball to help complete the r. Remove JTN, work in ends and trim.

Bead Streamers: Thread bead threader with 18 inches DMC #8. String one 4mm pearl bead. Remove threader, fold two ends of strand together, and rethread the bead threader. String one 6mm pearl bead, 14 pearl 4mm beads. Remove bead threader and attach streamers to bottom center r with tapestry needle and trim.

Repeat instructions for Bead Streamers twice, stringing 12 beads on each thread instead of 14.

Cut 8-inch piece of ribbon and tie to top of ball for hanging. Tie a bow around the stem with remaining ribbon.

Golden Elegance Christmas Ornament

Materials: JTN #00 and threader, tapestry needle and scissors, 6 yards gold DMC #8 pearl cotton for cc, 1/4 ball gold metallic thread, 21 pearl 4mm beads, 30 pearl 2.5mm beads, one pearl 10mm bead, bead threader, 1 egg-shaped pink satin ball, 1 toothpick.

String 21 pearl 4mm beads onto metallic gold thread and push them down into the ball.

Rnd 1: Thread JTN with 2 yards DMC #8 for cc. Start with the bottom round in the ornament and tat with metallic thread. R of 3 ds, 3 p sep by 3 ds, 3 ds, sson, clr. Ch 8 dsb, 1 two-finger p, 8 dsb, sson.

*R of 3 ds, j to last p of previous r, 5 ds, s-1b, 5 ds, p, 3 ds, sson, clr. Ch 8 dsb, 1 two-finger p, 8 dsb, sson. R of 3 ds, j to last p of previous r, 3 ds, p, 3 ds, p, 3 ds, sson, clr. Ch 8 dsb, 1 two-finger p, 8 dsb, sson. Repeat from * 5 times. R of 3 ds, j to last p of previous r, 5 ds, s-1b, 5 ds, j to first p of first r at beginning of rnd (bring r around as if to clasp a necklace). Ch 3 ds, sson, clr. Ch 8 dsb, 1 two-finger p, 8 dsb, sson. J ch to base of first r, rnr. Remove JTN, work in ends and trim.

Rnd 2: Thread JTN with 1-3/4 yards DMC #8 for cc. *R of 10 ds, j to middle p of any small r in previous rnd, 10 ds, sson, clr. Ch 12 dsb, s-1b, sson. Repeat from * 6 times. J last ch to base of first r, rnr. Remove JTN, work in ends and trim.

Rnd 3: Thread JTN with 1-3/4 yards DMC #8 for cc. *R of 8 ds, pick up previous rnd, right side out and j to bp in any ch as follows: Insert JTN under bead in p from back, drawing ball strand across front of bp from right to left under the JTN. With tip of JTN, catch ball strand and draw a loop out of p as if to purl a stitch. Leave loop on JTN. Fold bead toward you and down. Give ball strand a tug from the left side of the bead to tighten bp against the JTN, ch 8 ds, sson, clr.

Ch 12 dsb, s-1b, 12 dsb, sson. Repeat from * 6 times. J last ch to base of first r, rnr. Remove JTN, work in ends and trim.

Gathering Bottom Picots into a Center Ring: Thread JTN with 21 inches DMC #8 for cc. R of 1 ds, j to p of any ch in first row (avoid twist in p), 2 ds, *j to next p. Repeat from * until all p have been connected. When joining the last p work near tip of JTN, sson, clr. Work in ends, 2 one direction and 2 the opposite. Trim carefully. Gently stretch picots to even them on ring.

Gathering Top Picots: Insert toothpick in bottom of egg and set aside. Thread bead threader with 21 inches metallic thread. "Sew" through the bead on every ch of top rnd. Slip tatting over the egg ball so that bottom ring is over the toothpick. Tie a half knot with the two ends and pull to gather the beads into a ring at top and to enclose the egg. Tie a knot, and with remaining thread tie ends to form a loop for hanging.

Bottom Trim: Thread bead threader with 18 inches DMC #8. String 15 pearl 2.5mm beads. String the 10mm pearl bead and remaining 15 pearl 2.5mm beads. Remove bead threader, tie ends to gather beads into a r, stitch to bottom center r and trim.

Southern Belle Christmas Ornament

Materials: JTN #000 and threader, tapestry needle and scissors, #8 steel crochet hook, 6-inch piece of wire for bead threader, needle-nose pliers, 18 straight pins, 1/2 ball rose DMC #8 pearl cotton, 15 yards white DMC #12 pearl cotton for cc, 1 yard 3/8-inch rose satin ribbon, 28 pearl 4mm beads, 196 pearl 2.5mm beads, 4 pearl 6mm x 9mm teardrops, one 2-1/2-inch diameter white satin ball, 5/8x2-inch piece of cardboard.

Center Band: Using JTN, thread end of ball strand and string 14 pearl 4mm beads and push them down into the ball. Remove JTN.

Rnd 1: Thread JTN with 3-1/2 yards white DMC #12 for cc. *R of 6 ds, p, 6 ds, p, 2 ds, 5 p sep by 2 ds, 2 ds, sson, clr. Ch 5 dsb, p, 2 dsb, p, 2 dsb, s-1b, 2 ds, p, 2 ds, p, 5 dsb, sson. J ch to second p in previous r, rnp. Ch 5 dsb, p, 2 dsb, p, 2 dsb, s-1b, 2 dsb, p, 2 dsb, p, 5 dsb, sson.

R of 2 ds, 4 p sep by 2 ds, 2 ds. J to p in previous r where ch are connected. Ch 6 ds, p, 6 ds, sson, clr. Repeat from * 6 times. J to base of first r, rnr to close the rnd. Remove JTN, work in ends and trim. Set aside.

Rnd 2: Thread JTN with 3 yards DMC #12 for cc. *R of 6 ds, pick up Rnd 1 and j to p at right of bp in any ch of previous rnd, 4 ds, p, 2 ds, sson, clr. R of 2 ds, j to last p of previous small r (use crochet hook to join), 4 ds. J to p at left of bead in next ch at right in previous rnd, 6 ds, sson, clr. Ch 6 dsb, 5 p sep by 2 dsb, 6 dsb, sson. Repeat from * 13 times. J ch to base of first small r at beginning of rnd, rnr. Remove JTN, work in ends and trim.

Upper Rnds and Stem Ring:
Rnd 1 — Beaded Rnd: Thread JTN with one end of 1-1/4 yards DMC #8. Attach by tying opposite end to any p in any large r in first rnd of center band.
*String 6 pearl 2.5mm beads. Working from left to right along top edge of center band, backstitch into p of next r with JTN and secure beads between p. Repeat from * working in six beads each time until all p have been attached with beads. End the rnd by taking a backstitch into the first p and beginning of rnd. Remove JTN, work ends into r of previous rnd and trim.

Rnd 2: Thread JTN with 2-1/4 yards DMC #12 for cc. Attach cc between two middle beads of any beaded ch in previous rnd by running JTN through the beaded ch, through loop of cc, and securing between the 2 middle beads.
*Ch 12 dsb, p, 3 dsb. Using cardboard, make a 5/8-inch mp. Ch 3 dsb, p, 12 dsb, sson. J to p in next ch at left, rnp. Repeat from * 13 times, ending by joining to the first p at beginning of rnd. Remove JTN, work in ends and trim.

Top of Stem Ring: Thread JTN with 30 inches DMC #12 for cc. Slip loop end over right little finger until you are ready to close the ring. R of 1 ds, using the piece of wire *string 1 pearl 4mm bead onto middle p in any ch of previous rnd. Run JTN through p, remove wire, 2 ds. Repeat from * 13 times, 1 ds, sson, clr. Remove JTN, work in ends and trim.

Lower Rnds: Turn work upside down. Thread JTN with one end of 1-1/2 yards DMC #8. Tie opposite end to any middle p of any ch in lower rnd of band.
*String 8 pearl 2.5mm beads and take a backstitch into middle p of next ch to right. Repeat from * 13 times. End by taking a backstitch with the JTN into the first p at beginning of rnd. Remove JTN, work ends into tatted ch and trim.

Bottom Ring: Slip tatting over satin ball so that the top r fits over the stem. Stretch the work down around the ball.

Insert straight pin through small r of each motif to hold the work on the ball. Insert toothpick into center bottom of ball. Thread JTN with 30 inches DMC #12 for cc. Slip loop end over the toothpick until you are ready to close the ring. Ch 1 ds, *j between two middle beads of bead ch in previous rnd, 2 ds. Repeat from * 13 times, 1 ds, sson, clr.

You may need to slide a few ds at a time to close this ring. The ring will be wide (about 1/2 inch in diameter). Remove JTN and trim. Cut ball strand 25 inches from work. Thread this end in tapestry needle. Take a few stitches to secure the r and sew a crisscross in the r. Do not pull r. Work in ends and trim.

Ribbon Streamers: Cut two 8-inch pieces of ribbon. Using JTN and thread, pull one end of ribbon through any bar of the crisscross at bottom of ball. Remove JTN and thread. Using tapestry needle and DMC #8, sew a teardrop to one end of ribbon. Repeat for other ribbon end. Attach second ribbon by pulling it through the crisscross bar opposite the first ribbon.

Straighten ribbons to even with satin on outside when ball is hung. Tack both ribbons at crisscross to secure and trim carefully. Cut 6-inch piece of ribbon and attach it to the stem for hanging. Tie a bow around the stem with remaining ribbon.

Mary's Snowflake

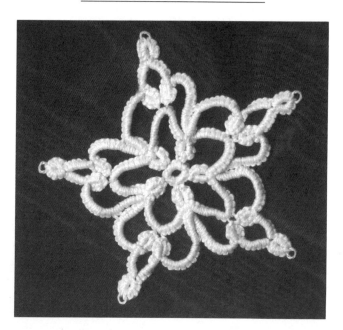

Materials: JTN #0 and threader, embroidery needle and scissors, 1/4 ball of white DMC #3 pearl cotton, 3-inch-square piece of cardboard.

Measurement: Snowflake measures 5 inches wide.

Center Ring: Thread JTN with 18 inches DMC #3 for cc. R of 1 ds, 5 p sep by 2 ds, 1 ds, sson, clr. Remove JTN, work in ends and trim.

Rnd 1: Thread JTN with 1-1/2 yards thread for cc. *R of 3 ds, pick up center r (knot side facing), j to any p, 3 ds, sson, clr. Ch 8 dsb, p, 8 dsb, sson. Repeat from * 4 times. J last ch to base of first r, rnr. Remove JTN, work ends into base of r and trim.

Rnd 2: Thread JTN with 3 yards thread for cc. *R of 3 ds, j to p on any ch of previous rnd (be sure knot side is facing). Ch 3 ds, sson, clr. Ch 6 dsb, sson. R of 4 dsb, p, 4 dsb, sson, clr. Ch 6 dsb,

sson.

Look at snowflake, knot side up, to be sure chains are not twisted. R of 3 ds, j to same p in ch of first rnd. Avoid twist in p, 3 ds, sson, clr. Ch 9 dsb, p, 5 dsb, sson. Run JTN through center of next r in first rnd, between strands of cc, and secure at base of r, rnr. Turn work clockwise, bringing cc toward you, under ball strand and across top of work. Ch 5 dsb, j to p in previous ch at left, 9 dsb, sson. Turn work clockwise, bringing cc to back of work. Repeat from * 4 times, j last ch to base of first r, rnr. Remove JTN, work in ends and trim.

Stiffening the Snowflake: For a firm snowflake, wet sponge with a mixture of starch and water and pat on snowflake. Place snowflake on Turkish towel right side down and allow to dry. Place cotton cloth over snowflake and press with iron.

Louise's Snowflake

Materials: JTN #0 and threader, tapestry needle and scissors, one ball white DMC #3 pearl cotton.

Measurement: 4 inches in diameter

Thread JTN with 3-1/2 yards thread for cc. *R of 6 ds, p, 4 ds, p, 2 ds, sson, clr. Ch 1 dsb, sson. R of 2 ds, j to last p of previous r, 10 ds, p, 2 ds, p, 10 ds, p, 2 ds, sson, clr. Ch 1 dsb, sson. R of 2 ds, j to last p in previous r, 4 ds, p, 6 ds, sson, clr – first clover complete. Ch 3 dsb, 8 p sep by 2 dsb, 3 dsb, sson.

*R of 3 ds, j to last p in last r of previous clover, 6 ds, p, 3 ds, sson, clr. Ch 3 dsb, 8 p sep by 2 ds, 3 dsb, sson. R of 6 ds, j to last p of previous r, 4 ds, p, 2 ds, sson, clr. Ch 1 dsb, sson. R of 2 ds, j to last p of previous r, 10 ds. J to right

center p of previous large r, 2 ds, p, 10 ds, p, 2 ds, sson, clr. Ch 1 dsb, sson. R of 2 ds, j to last p of previous r, 4 ds, p, 6 ds, sson, clr.

Turn work clockwise, bringing cc toward you, under ball strand and across previous r. Ch 3 dsb, j to p in ch at left, 2 dsb, 7 p sep by 2 dsb, 3 dsb, sson.

Repeat from * 3 times except j 2nd center p of last large r of last clover to first p of large r of first clover. R of 3 ds, j to last p of previous r, 3 ds, p, 3 ds, j to p in first r of first clover, 3 ds, sson, clr. Ch 3 dsb, 7 p sep by 2 dsb, 2 dsb, fold first clover away from you, j to p in first ch of that clover, 3 dsb, sson. J ch to first r of clover, rnr. Remove JTN, work in ends and trim.

Jenny's Snowflake

Materials: JTN #0 and threader, yarn needle and scissors, ball of white DMC #3 pearl cotton.

Inner Rnd: Thread JTN with 1-1/2 yards DMC #3 for cc. R of 2 ds, 3 p sep by 5 ds, 2 ds, sson, clr. Ch 6 dsb, sson.

*R of 2 ds, j to last p of previous r, 5 ds, p, 5 ds, p, 2 ds, sson, clr. Ch 6 dsb, sson. Repeat from * 3 times. R of 2 ds, j to last p of previous r, 5 ds, p, 5 ds, bring first r around and j to first p as if to clasp a necklace, 2 ds, sson, clr. Ch 6 dsb, sson. J to base of first r, rnr. Re-move JTN, work in ends and trim.

Outer Rnd: Thread JTN with 2-1/2 yards thread for cc. *R of 7 ds, j to mid-dle p of any r in inner rnd (be sure knot side of p is facing), 2 ds, p, 5 ds, sson, clr. Ch 3 dsb, 3 p sep by 3 dsb, 3 dsb, sson.

R of 5 dsb, j to last p of previous r, 2 ds, j to same p in same r of inner rnd, 7 ds, sson, clr. Ch 3 dsb, 3 p sep by 3 dsb, 3 dsb, sson. Repeat from * 5 times. J last ch to base of first r, rnr. Remove JTN, work in ends and trim.

Teresa's Snowflake

This snowflake measures 4-1/2 inches in diameter.

Materials: JTN #0 and threader, embroidery needle and scissors, 1/4 ball DMC #3 pearl cotton.

Inner Motif: Thread JTN with 1-1/2 yards DMC #3 for cc. R of 2 ds, 5 p sep by 2 ds, 2 ds, sson, clr. Do not cut thread. Working counterclockwise around r, 6 dsb, p, 6 dsb, sson. J to p, rnp to left (right side is facing).

*Ch 1 dsb, p, 6 dsb, sson. J rnp to next p in r. Repeat from * 4 times, last ch will be j to base of center r, rnr. Remove JTN, work in ends and trim.

Outer Round: Thread JTN with 3 yards DMC #3 for cc. Attach to p in any ch of center motif by running JTN up

p, through loop of cc, and securing cc to the p over ch.

Working clockwise around center motif, *ch 4 ds, p, 2 ds, sson. R of 2 ds, j to p of previous ch, 4 ds, p, 2 ds, sson, clr. Ch 1 dsb, sson. R of 2 ds, j to last p of previous r, 4 ds, p, 4 ds, p, 2 ds, sson, clr. Ch 1 dsb, sson. R of 2 ds, j to last p of previous r, 4 ds, p, 2 ds, sson, clr. Ch 2 ds, j to last p of previous r, 4 ds, sson. (Be sure right side of center motif is facing.) J rnp to p in ch at right in center motif. Repeat from * 5 times. Remove JTN, work in ends and trim.

To launder, follow instructions on DMC label. When dry, spray wet sponge with liquid starch and pat snowflake to stiffen. Press if needed.

Teddy's Beaded North Star

Materials: JTN #0 and threader, embroidery needle and scissors, bead threader, one skein DMC #3 pearl cotton, 42 white pearl 6mm beads.

String 42 beads on ball strand with bead threader, pushing them down into ball.

Thread JTN with 1-1/2 yards DMC #3 for cc. R of 1 ds, s-1b, *1 ds, p, 1 ds, s-1b. Repeat from * 4 times, 1 ds, sson.

Rnd 1: Working counterclockwise around center r, *8 dsb, slide 3 beads (s-3b) up to JTN, 8 dsb, sson. J to p between next two beads at left of ch, rnp. (Be sure right side of r is facing.) Repeat from * 5 times, j to last ch of base of r, rnr. Remove JTN, work in ends and trim.

Rnd 2: Thread JTN with 1-1/2 yards DMC #3 for cc. Attach cc to any p of previous rnd over ch by running JTN through p, through loop of cc, and securing to p. Ch 3 dsb, p, 7 dsb, sson. Work counterclockwise around star with right side facing. J to 3 bp (point) at left between first two beads, rnp. Ch 5 dsb,

s-3b, 5 dsb, sson. J to same inner beaded point between 2nd and 3rd beads, rnp. Ch 7 dsb, p, 3 dsb, sson. J to next p in center r over ch of previous rnd, rnp.

*Turn work clockwise, bringing cc toward you, under ball strand and across center r. Ch 3 dsb, j to last p of previous ch at left, 7 dsb, sson. Turn work counterclockwise, bringing cc to back of work. J to next 3 bp (point) between first two beads, rnp. Ch 5 dsb, s-3b, 5 dsb, sson. J to same inner beaded point between last 2 beads, rnp. Ch 7 ds, p, 3 ds, sson. J to next p on center r over ch of previous rnd, rnp. Repeat from * 4 times, sson last ch after 7 dsb sts. Fold first point of star away, then back, rnp the first p of the first ch, 3 dsb, sson. J to base of center r, rnr. Remove JTN, work in ends and trim.

Use fabric stiffener to starch. Blot excess starch with towel. Use soft toothbrush to remove excess starch around double stitches and beads. Allow to dry.

Holiday Cutouts

There are no specific patterns given for these holiday cutouts. Make a selection of an animal, bird, star or any other object from a book or freehand a design. With a soft lead pencil, trace outline on felt (or fabric desired) for cutout. Decorate cutouts with tatted rings, chains and beads using Jiffy Tatting Needles with recommended threads or yarns.

Cut two pattern pieces (one for back,

the other for front), embroider features on front piece. Fuse front and back pieces together with Stitch Witchery™. Use the Jiffy Tatting Needle as a needle to attach tatting as it is being worked. Add tatting to front or to both sides of cutout and use as ornaments or package decorations for special occasions.

Christmas Tree Note Card

This tree measures 1 x 1-1/2 inches.

Materials: JTN #000 and threader, embroidery needle and scissors, 1-1/2 yards white DMC #12 pearl cotton for cc, 3 yards green DMC #8 for ball strand.

Thread JTN with 1-1/2 yards white DMC #12 for cc.

Right Side of Tree: Start at right lower large ring. R of 8 ds, p, 4 ds, p, 4 ds, sson,

clr. Ch 3 dsb, 5 p sep by 2 dsb, 2 dsb, sson. R of 3 ds, j to last p of previous r, 3 ds, p, 3 ds, p, 3 ds, sson, clr. Ch 3 dsb, 3 p sep by 2 dsb, 2 dsb, sson.

R of 2 ds, j to last p of previous r, 2 ds, p (this is the anchor picot that holds the top), 4 ds, sson, clr. Ch 3 dsb, 3 p sep by 2 dsb, 2 dsb, sson. Run JTN through last anchor p of previous r, between

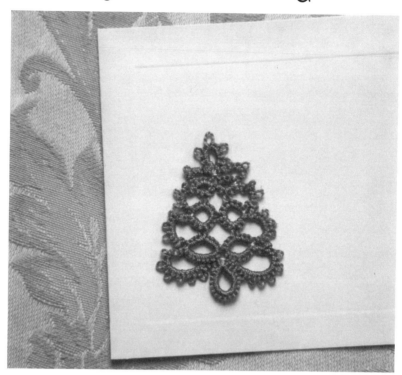

strands of cc, and secure ch in place on p. Avoid distorting p – right side complete.

Top of Tree: Turn tree clockwise (ch are on left and back of tree is facing). Bring ball strand toward you, under cc and across back of work. R of 2 dsb, j to p of previous ch, 2 dsb, 3 p sep by 2 dsb, 2 dsb, sson, clr. This r is made with dsb because you are working at back of tree. Do not turn.

Run JTN through anchor p of previous r where previous ch was connected, back through strands of cc to secure top r. With the back of tree facing, 2 dsb, j to last p of previous r (top ring), sson – top of tree complete. Turn tree upside down with right side facing.

Left Side of Tree: R of 4 ds, j to anchor p in opposite r where top r and top ch are connected, 2 ds, p, 2 ds, sson, clr. Ch 2 dsb, 3 p sep by 2 ds, 3 dsb, sson. R of

3 ds, j to last p of previous r, 3 ds, j to middle p of opposite r, 3 ds, p, 3 ds, sson, clr. Ch 2 dsb, 5 p sep by 2 ds, 3 dsb, sson. R of 4 ds, j to last p of previous r, 4 ds, j to middle p of opposite r, 8 ds, sson, clr – left side complete.

Lower Branches and Tree Trunk: Ch 2 dsb, 8 p sep by 2 dsb, 2 dsb, sson (avoid bunching knots). Run JTN through p between 2 lower r of tree, through strands of cc, and secure ch to p. Turn tree clockwise, back facing. Tree is still upside down. Pull cc toward you, under ball strand and across tree. R of 2 dsb, j to last p of previous ch, 16 dsb, p, 2 dsb, sson, clr.

Working at back of tree, ch 2 dsb, j to last p of previous r, 8 p sep by 2 dsb, 2 dsb, sson. Turn tree upright. Run JTN up center of first r, between strands of cc and secure to base of r. Remove JTN, work in ends and trim.

Floppy Bunny Note Card

Materials: JTN #000 and threader, embroidery needle and scissors, 1-1/2 yards DMC #12 pearl cotton, 3 yards DMC #8, 2 yards contrasting color thread for tail and bow.

Head: Thread JTN with 24 inches DMC #12 for cc. Leaving a 3-inch length of the 3 yards DMC #8, tat a r of 4 ds, 3 half hitches (hh) of just the first half of ds for nose, 9 ds. Make 2 one-finger p for tiny ears. Ch 4 ds, p, 3 ds, sson, clr. Do not cut cc. Work in 3-inch length with embroidery needle and trim.

Body: R of 3 ds, j to last p of head, 9 ds, 1 tp to mark point for tail, 9 ds. Make two longer tp, one right after the other, about 1/2 inch long when open on JTN for paws, 6 ds, sson, clr. Avoid bunching ds. Work in ends and trim.

Tail and Bow: Make a Josephine Knot (jk) for the tail. Thread JTN with 18 inches DMC #12 for cc. R of 9 shh for jk, sson, clr. With ends of thread and embroidery needle, attach to tp on body. Tie a bow around the neck. A contrasting color can be used for the bow if desired. Attach Floppy Bunny to a note card.

Sweetheart Note Card

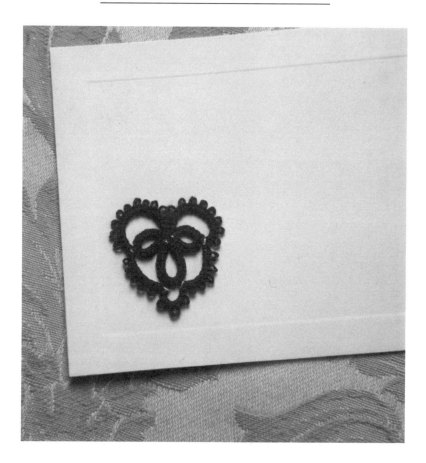

Materials: JTN #000 and threader, embroidery needle and scissors, 24 inches white DMC #12 pearl cotton for cc, 2 yards red DMC #8 pearl cotton.

Clover: Thread JTN with DMC #12 for cc. R of 8 ds, p, 6 ds, p, 2 ds, sson, clr. R of 2 ds, j to last p of previous r, 9 ds, p, 2 ds, p, 9 ds, p, 2 ds, sson, clr. R of 2 ds, j to last p of previous r, 6 ds, p, 8 ds, sson, clr.

Border for Heart: Ch 6 dsb, 9 p sep by 2 dsb, 3 dsb, sson. Attach to p of left r

of clover (be sure right side of clover is facing). Run JTN up p, between strands of cc, rnp. Ch 2 dsb, 7 p sep by 2 dsb, 2 dsb, sson. J to next p, rnp. Ch 2 dsb, 3 p sep by 2 dsb, 2 dsb, sson. J to next p, rnp.

Ch 2 dsb, 5 p sep by 2 dsb, 2 dsb, sson. J to next p, rnp. Ch 3 dsb, 9 p sep by 2 dsb, 6 dsb, sson. J to base of right r in clover, rnr. Remove JTN, sew in ends and trim. Attach to note card.

On Wings of Love Heart

Materials: JTN #0, tapestry needle and scissors, threader, one ball red DMC #3 thread.

Center Butterfly Motif: Thread JTN with 1 yard DMC #3 for cc. Start with right large wing. R of 2 ds, p, 7 ds, p, 6 ds, p, 7 ds, p, 2 ds, sson, clr. R of 2 ds, j to last p of previous r, 6 ds, p, 6 ds, p, 2 ds, sson, clr. R of 2 ds, j to last p of previous r, 6 ds, p, 6 ds, p, 2 ds, sson, clr. R of 2 ds, j to last p of previous r, 7 ds, p, 6 ds, p, 7 ds, p, 2 ds, sson, clr. Remove JTN, work in ends and trim.

Heart Motif: Thread JTN with 2-1/4 yards thread for cc. With right side facing, run JTN through first p on inside edge of each large wing, through loop of cc, and secure cc to the two p.

Ch 6 dsb, sson. R of 3 ds, j to first p in large left wing, 3 ds, p, 6 ds, sson, clr. Ch 10 dsb, sson. J to last p of previous r by running JTN up p, between strands of cc, and securing to p (rnp). R of 6 dsb, p, 6 dsb, sson, clr. Ch 10 dsb, sson, j to last p of previous r, rnp. R of 3 ds, j to next p in same large wing, 3 ds, p, 6 ds, sson, clr. Ch 10 dsb, sson, j to last p of previous r, rnp.

R of 6 ds, p, 6 ds, sson, clr. Ch 10 dsb, sson. J to last p of previous r, rnp. R of 3 ds, j to p in small left wing, 3 ds, p, 6 ds, sson, clr. Ch 10 dsb, sson, j to last p of previous r, rnp.

R of 4 ds, p, 2 ds, p, 6 ds, sson, clr. Ch 8 dsb, p, 2 dsb, sson. J to last p of previous r, rnp. Turn heart clockwise, bringing cc toward you, to right across top of work. At bottom point of back of heart, r of 2 ds, j to last p in previous ch, 6 dsb, p, 6 dsb, p, 2 dsb, sson, clr. Turn work counterclockwise, bringing cc to back of heart. R of 2 ds, j to p in next to last r at left, 4 ds, p, 6 dsb, sson, clr.

Turn work clockwise, bringing cc toward you across previous r. Ch 2 dsb,

j to last p in point r, 8 dsb, sson.

Turn work counterclockwise, j to last p of previous r, rnp. R of 3 ds, j to p in right small wing, 3 ds, p, 6 ds, sson, clr. Ch 10 dsb, sson. J to last p of previous r, rnp.

R of 6 ds, p, 6 ds, sson, clr. Ch 10 dsb, sson, j to last p in previous r, rnp. R of 3 ds, j to first p in large right wing, 3 ds, p, 6 ds, sson, clr. Ch 10 dsb, sson. J to last p in previous r, rnp.

R of 6 ds, p, 6 ds, sson, clr. Ch 10 dsb, sson, j to last p of previous r, rnp. R of 3 ds, j to next p in large right wing, 3 ds, p, 6 ds, sson, clr. Ch 10 dsb, sson.

Run JTN up center of previous r, between strands of cc. Before securing, open last p in that r and secure cc over open p. Ch 6 dsb, sson, j ch to same two p where cc was attached at beginning of rnd, rnp. Remove JTN, work in ends and trim.

Valentine Heart

Materials: JTN #00 and threader, embroidery needle and scissors, 2-1/2 yards red DMC #8 for cc, 7 yards red DMC #5 for tatting.

Measurement: 2-3/4 x 3 inches

Thread JTN with 2-1/2 yards DMC #8 for cc. Leaving a 4-inch length of DMC #5, begin with clover at crease of heart, r of 5 ds, 5 p sep by 2 ds, 4 ds, p, 2 ds, sson, clr. Work in end length with embroidery needle, ch 1 dsb, sson.

R of 2 ds, j to last p of previous r, *8 ds, p, 2 ds, repeat from * once, sson, clr. Ch 1 dsb, sson.

R of 2 ds, j to last p of previous r, 4 ds, 5 p sep by 2 ds, 5 ds, sson, clr — clover complete. Do not cut thread.

Ch 12 dsb, sson. R of 6 ds, j to first p at left r of clover (knot side is right side), 3 ds, p, 3 ds, sson, clr. Ch 12 dsb, sson.

*R of 3 ds, j to last p of previous r, 3 ds, j to next p on same r of clover, 3 ds, p, 3 ds, sson, clr. Ch 12 dsb, sson. Repeat from * 3 times.

R of 3 ds, j to last p of previous r, 3 ds, j to first p in middle r of clover, 3 ds, p, 3 ds, sson, clr. Ch 10 dsb, p, 2 dsb, sson. R of 6 ds, j to p of previous r, 2 ds, p, 6 ds, sson, clr.

Turn heart over so completed side is on left (heart is upside down), bring cc forward, drawing it across back of previous r.

R of 2 dsb, j to last p of previous ch, 16 dsb, p, 2 dsb, sson, clr. Ch 2 dsb, j to last p of previous r, 10 dsb, sson — bottom point of heart complete. Turn heart right side facing (point of heart at bottom).

R of 3 ds, j to last p of previous r (inside point of heart), 3 ds, j to second p in middle r of clover, 3 ds, p, 3 ds, sson, clr. Ch 12 dsb, sson.

*R of 3 ds, j to last p of previous r, 3 ds, j to first p in right r of clover, 3 ds, p, 3 ds, sson, clr. Ch 12 dsb, sson. Repeat from * 3 times, j to next p in right r of clover.

R of 3 ds, j to last p of previous r, 3 ds, j to last p in same r of clover, 6 ds, sson, clr. Ch 12 dsb, sson. Run JTN up through center of right r of clover, between strands of cc, and secure cc at base of r.

Remove JTN, sew cc ends into ch and other end into r of clover and trim. Attach a tie of same thread or of ribbon to center r at crease of heart to hang or attach to package.

Bible Cross Bookmark

Materials: JTN #00 and threader, tapestry needle and scissors, 1 ball DMC #5 pearl cotton, 1/4 ball DMC #8 in same color for cc.

Dimensions: 5 x 6-1/4 inches

Body of Cross: Start at the inner ring at foot of cross and work up right side. Thread JTN with 3 yards DMC #8 yarn for cc. R of 2 ds, 3 p sep by 2 ds, 4 ds, p, 4 ds, sson, clr. Ch 10 dsb, sson. *R of 4 ds, j to last p of previous r, 4 ds, tp, 4 ds, p, 4 ds, sson, clr. Ch 10 dsb, sson.

Repeat from * 7 times. R of 4 ds, j to last p of previous r, 4 ds, tp, 3 p sep by 2 ds, 2 ds, sson, clr. Do not cut thread.

Crest for Head of Cross: (a) Ch 16 dsb, sson. R of 8 ds, j to last p of previous inner r, 4 ds, p, 4 ds, sson, clr. Ch 12 dsb, sson. R of 4 ds, j to last p of previous r, 4 ds, j to next p in inner r, 4 ds, p, 4 ds, sson, clr. Ch 12 dsb, sson. R of 4 ds, j to last p of previous r, 4 ds, j to next p in inner r, 8 ds, sson, clr. Ch 16 dsb, sson.

previous r, 4 ds, tp, 4 ds, p, 4 ds, sson, clr. Ch 10 dsb, sson. R of 4 ds, j to last p of previous r, 4 ds, tp, 3 p sep by 2 ds, 2 ds, sson, clr. Do not cut thread.

Crest for Right Arm: Repeat Crest for Head of Cross (a), (b). *Ch 10 dsb, sson. Attach ch to tp in next r on r opposite base of r. Repeat from * once. Ch 1 dsb, sson. Attach to 3rd ch from top inner r as before. Remove JTN, work in ends and trim.

Left Arm of Cross: Turn cross upside down. Repeat Right Arm of Cross, starting at 3rd right chain up from inner ring at head of cross. End by attaching to 6th right ch from foot of cross. Remove JTN, work in ends and trim.

Chain Border: Thread JTN with 4 yards thread for cc. Attach to base of inner r at foot of cross by running JTN through center of r and loop of cc, securing at base of r.

Working up right lower side of body, *ch 12 dsb, attach to base of next r, rnr. Repeat from * 4 times, ch 6 dsb, sson. Attach to base of 3rd r from inner r of right arm.

Working around right arm, *ch 12 dsb, sson. Attach to base of next r, rnr. Repeat from * once. Ch 20 dsb, sson, attach to base of next r, rnr in crest.

*Ch 16 dsb, sson. Attach to base of next r. Repeat from * once. Ch 20 dsb, sson. Attach to base of next r, rnp (inner ring). *Ch 12 dsb, sson. Attach to next r, rnp. Repeat from * once, ch 6 dsb, sson. Attach to base of 3rd r from inner r at top of cross, rnr.

Chain Around Top of Cross: Repeat instructions for Chain Border of Right Arm.

Chain Around Left Arm: Repeat instructions for Chain Border of Right Arm, working down left side of lower body. *Ch 12 dsb, attach to next r, rnp. Repeat from * 4 times. Ch 20 dsb, sson, attach to base of next r, rnr in crest. Remove JTN, work in ends and trim. Stretch cross lightly to straighten chains and block.

(b) Attach ch to inner r at tp by inserting JTN through center of inner r, between strands of cc, and securing to edge of r opposite base of same r. This completes the crest. Do not cut thread.

Opposite Side Chains in Body of Cross: *Ch 10 dsb, sson. Attach to next r as in (b) above. Repeat from * 8 times, attach last ch to inner r at foot of cross, rnp. The work will curve, but will straighten when cross is completed. Do not cut thread.

Crest at Foot of Cross: Turn cross upside down. Repeat Crest for Head of Cross (a). Remove JTN, work in ends and trim.

Right Arm of Cross: Thread JTN with 2 yards thread for cc. Attach cc to 6th ch from inner r at foot of cross by running JTN through ch, through loop of cc, and securing cc in place in center of ch. Ch 1 dsb, sson.

R of 8 ds, tp, 4 ds, p, 4 ds, sson, clr. Ch 10 dsb, sson. R of 4 ds, j to last p of

HOLIDAY COLLECTION

INDEX

OTHER BOOKS FROM
THE CLASSIC COLLECTION

Jiffy Needle Tatting – Exciting Fashion Accessories	$8.95
Jiffy Needle Tatting – A to Z	$8.95
Jiffy Needle Tatting – Quick & Easy	$8.95
Tatting Patterns	$6.95
Collars to Knit and Crochet	$6.95
Afghans to Crochet	$7.95
U.S. State Quilt Blocks	$6.95

To order any of these books, have your credit card ready
and call toll-free 1-800-678-8025
or write WORKBASKET Books & Products,
P.O. Box 11230, Des Moines, IA 50340.